THE MONSTER BUTLER

Also available from Black & White Publishing by A. M. Nicol

MANUEL: SCOTLAND'S FIRST SERIAL KILLER

THE MONSTER BUTLER
INSIDE THE MIND OF A SERIAL KILLER

A. M. NICOL
Foreword by Paul McBride QC

BLACK & WHITE PUBLISHING

First published 2011
by Black & White Publishing Ltd
29 Ocean Drive, Edinburgh EH6 6JL

1 3 5 7 9 10 8 6 4 2 11 12 13 14

ISBN: 978 1 84502 336 2

Copyright © A. M. Nicol 2011

The publisher has made every reasonable effort to contact
copyright holders of images in the picture section. Any errors are
inadvertent and anyone who, for any reason, has not been contacted
is invited to write to the publisher so that a full acknowledgment
can be made in subsequent editions of this work.

A CIP catalogue record for this book
is available from the British Library.

Typeset by Ellipsis Books Limited, Glasgow
Printed and bound by MPG Books Ltd, Bodmin, Cornwall

CONTENTS

PART II:
THE REAL ROY FONTAINE

PART III:
THE MAKING OF A MONSTER

ACKNOWLEDGEMENTS

I am grateful to Mirian and Moray; to Paul for providing the Foreword; to the staff at the National Archives, Edinburgh, and the Mitchell Library, Glasgow, and to all at Black & White Publishing.

FOREWORD

by PAUL McBRIDE QC

Over the years, Scotland has produced serial killers from Manuel to Tobin and, gruesome as their crimes may have been, they have always caught the imagination of a public hungry for information as to how ordinary people from seemingly normal backgrounds can go on to commit the vilest of crimes.

A. M. Nicol, a very talented advocate, has now turned his forensic skills to studying a man from humble beginnings who was born in Partick in 1924, originally as Archibald Hall, but who later became known as Roy Fontaine, the serial killer who murdered not only his own brother but four other people apparently for gain, glamour and possibly pleasure.

In this detailed investigation, Nicol charts how Archibald Hall briefly became a butler to some of the finest gentlemen in society and studied in intricate detail the etiquette of polite society and their accents and protocol, all with a view to ultimately lining his own pockets. Hall was undoubtedly a formidable personality with the ability to lie, cheat and steal.

However, the real question in this fascinating insight into a deranged individual is how he became an uncaring serial killer. With impeccable research both north and south of the border, Nicol strips away the layers of this complicated man to reveal the dedication, obsession and greed that drove him to become the notorious individual we now know him to be.

The Monster Butler is a must read for anyone interested in human nature, the psychology of killers, the legal process and the parts of this country's history that many people would rather forget. This book deals with the age-old question of whether someone is merely fulfilling a predetermined destiny set in the stars, or whether a combination of circumstances or indeed the nature of evil itself were all factors that gave rise to this most unusual, refined, clever, enigmatic, flawed but ultimately heartless murderer.

This is a book not only of history and of human interest, but its message is also relevant to the times in which we currently live, as we are continually faced with the inexplicable cruelty of the criminal mind.

Impeccable research, clear narrative and logical analysis are the hallmarks of this excellent work but most of all it is a simply stunning read.

INTRODUCTION
A PLACE IN HISTORY

In 1919, the fifteen victorious allies of the Great War struck their own similar versions of a bronze medal called the Victory Medal. Any curiosity from the generations to come as to what had been at stake during the conflict can be easily answered: the reverse of the British version of the medal declares it had been 'The Great War For Civilisation 1914–1919'.

Civilisation, no less, had been at stake and the sacrifice of millions ensured that the fragile blossoming of human development, as seen through western eyes at the time, continued on its random way. But how is 'civilisation' judged?

In 1924, in Chicago, Illinois, the 'civilised' world was forced to come to terms with unexplained barbarity in its own ranks when it emerged that two highly intelligent teenagers from wealthy backgrounds, Leopold and Loeb, had planned and carried out the murder of fourteen-year-old Bobby Franks for only one possible reason – fun.

Attempting to stop his clients' executions, the famous lawyer Clarence Darrow addressed the court for twelve hours, and the judge decided not to impose death sentences, due in part to the ages of the killers. The judge also said:

> Life imprisonment, at the moment, strikes the public imagination as forcibly as would death by hanging, but to the offenders, particularly of the type they are, the prolonged

suffering of years of confinement may well be the severest form of retribution and expiation.

A civilised response to a barbaric act? To this day, the debate about executing murderers, or at least some of the more cold-blooded of them, continues.

That same year, a serial killer who was at least as ruthless as the two Chicago teenagers was born in Scotland.

After twenty-two-year-old Mary McMillan and twenty-eight-year-old Archibald Thomson Hall were married, their son was born in a flat in what was then called MacLean Street in the Partick area of Glasgow on 17 July 1924.

The boy was called Archibald Thomson Hall after his father and grandfather but would become better known as serial killer Roy Fontaine – 'The Monster Butler'. Fontaine must surely be one of the strangest characters to emerge in recent British criminal history, an area not lacking in odd individuals.

Apart from murdering five people, including Donald, his younger brother by nearly seventeen years, and spending most of his life in prison, where he died in 2002, Fontaine stands out for other reasons – he published his life story *A Perfect Gentleman* in 1999, later published as *To Kill and Kill Again* after his death; even Moors Murderer Myra Hindley failed to get *her* autobiography published. Moreover, there cannot be many who have been given life sentences for murder in both Scotland and England in the same year.

Whilst some offenders prefer to hide from the glare of publicity, Fontaine positively basked in it. He was far more encouraged than embarrassed by the media reaction to his murder convictions in 1978 and quickly tried to start a bidding war for his story. He courted as many journalists as he could to interest them in his own account of events and even encouraged relatives to cash in by telling what it was like to know him.

That said, it would have been difficult for Fontaine in particular not to have revelled in the sort of stuff being written in crime magazines – more in hope of sales than anything else – such as:

> He was a connoisseur of fine wines, an expert in antiques and a consummate actor. After spending most of his life in prison for jewellery thefts, he planned one more haul that would set him up in comfort for his old age. But his willingness to kill destroyed him.

From then on, he crafted the 'cultured gentleman jewel thief' image he desired.

When serving out his final jail sentence, he also 'demanded' elective state euthanasia for prisoners serving 'natural life' – as he was – whilst at the same time keeping an anxious eye on the possibility of a return to capital punishment. For Fontaine, the worst thing was not to be noticed.

But why would a serial killer with so much to hide want people to know so much about him? What does it say about him, except that he clearly sought sympathy?

Certainly, if the cover of *A Perfect Gentleman* is to be believed, Fontaine was a rich rogue driven to murder in extreme circumstances. The cover blurb states:

> Roy Archibald Hall was born into the poverty of pre-war Glasgow in 1924. As an exceptionally successful con-man and jewel thief, he lived the luxurious life of a high-class criminal – easy money punctuated by occasional prison time – but at the age of fifty-four, the smooth talking butler murdered a homosexual who tried to blackmail him. Another four people, including his brother, would die at his hands.

Even allowing for exaggeration, 'occasional prison time' hardly encapsulates the actual time the 'exceptionally successful con-man and jewel thief' spent safely locked away from potential victims. He was deemed to be insane three times and was sentenced, in total, to over seventy years in prison *before* he received the 'natural life term' in November 1978, aged fifty-four.

Yet, he is perhaps not as notorious as he should be – given the outrages he committed – because his more serious crimes occurred between 1977 and 1978. At that time, British society was coming to terms with the string of murders attributed to the Yorkshire Ripper, later found out to have been committed by a man named Peter Sutcliffe, and when Fontaine was finally arrested in East Lothian in 1978, it was only a few months after the brutal rape and murder of two young girls from Edinburgh, later known as the 'World's End' murders, so his sudden flurry of murderous activity in both England and Scotland attracted less interest than might otherwise have been expected.

Fontaine spent the last twenty-four years of his life in prison trying to justify many of the crimes he had committed in a life-long criminal career and probably hoping for one last spell of freedom. He told of his powerful sexual magnetism *to both sexes* and of wealthy employers regretful at losing a head-of-household so in touch with their aristocratic ways. Clearly, he was desperate to be remembered as a likeable scoundrel who, nevertheless, was a talented, cultured man of principle. He saw his own life as the story of a fascinating eccentric, action-packed with tales of well-planned gem thefts, ingenious scams and constant sex.

Some in our civilised society could perhaps see some truth in Fontaine's viewpoint, the almost romantic story of a man who was a victim of the circumstances he was born into, who led an extraordinary life and pulled himself up from the gutter to experience the world of the privileged. Others only saw him as a misguided, cold, calculating killer who was both delusional and a menace to society. Fontaine, however, was determined that his legacy would be the romantic version and that the world would remember him as he wished.

Throughout his life in prison, Fontaine worked hard to convince the world of his more flattering version of events, repeatedly telling his story to any willing listener. With each telling, the stories grew more exaggerated and far-fetched, quickly obscuring any remaining traces of reality. Going to great lengths to woo journalists and writers, Fontaine managed to successfully publish several 'biographical' accounts and indeed other writers have unsuccessfully attempted to get to the heart of his criminal tales. Over the years, the lines have blurred between what Fontaine claimed and what is actually verifiable fact.

To unravel the truth about the man who came to be known as the Monster Butler, we first need to look at Fontaine's own account of his criminal and personal life. Part One examines his life and times, following how he recounted the events that led him down the criminal path to murder, with his own justifications for his actions. Parts Two and Three then evaluate Fontaine's claims in order to uncover the true story of his life, allowing us to finally get inside the mind of a serial killer and discover what really led Archibald Hall, aka Roy Fontaine, to become one of the most notorious criminals of his generation.

PART I:

'HOW I DID IT – BY THE BUTLER'

1

THE TALENTED MR FONTAINE

Roy Fontaine's own version of his story, as relayed in *A Perfect Gentleman*, begins with him recalling how different he was from other young men of his age, a realisation gained due to the attention he received from young girls eager to have sex with him. A good-looking boy, he was also bright, charming and bold enough to impress. According to Fontaine, his charming personality was even powerful enough to attract attention from those beyond his adolescent circle. He claimed his most memorable date as his sixteenth birthday in 1940, when a thirty-something friend of his mother called Anne Philips bought him a dinner jacket and took him for a candlelit Italian meal before seducing him in her bedroom. Fontaine decided that the force of his personality caused him to exude a powerful sexual magnetism, a fact further confirmed in his own mind when his family moved to Catterick army base later that year and he made the same impression on the local girls there. As he recalled, 'I knew how to make love and I was always asked back for more. This wasn't much different from living back in Glasgow!'

The stay at Catterick was short-lived, though. Fontaine described how, one day, without warning, his family's house was raided and officers seized a collection of German and Nazi memorabilia he had been gathering. The officers who conducted the search asked Fontaine if he admired Hitler; he simply replied that he thought Hitler had done a good job stabilising the German economy, but that was all. However, only two days later,

Fontaine's father was conveniently told that he was 'too old for the armed forces'.

After the family returned to Glasgow, Fontaine experienced an entirely different sexual encounter with a Polish freedom fighter who had arrived in Britain to prepare for the fight against Nazism. Captain Jackobosky had taken lodgings with the Hall family in Glasgow's West End and Fontaine was immediately taken with the young Pole's knowledge of culture. According to Fontaine, when Jackobosky complained that he found the bed in his room uncomfortable, Fontaine's mother Marion solved the issue by moving him into her son's double bed. It was to be Fontaine's introduction to homosexuality. He now 'had the best of both worlds' and the two young men spent as much time as possible dining in the best restaurants and visiting galleries and museums together.

By that time, young Fontaine had decided not to live a life of 'drudgery, boredom and hardship' like his father and countless others, but to follow the far more exciting path of stealing gems for a living. He explained: 'I had a lascivious appreciation of jewels and fine antiques, just holding jewels made my cock hard. I would steal beautiful jewels from rich people. It was a conscious career decision.'

From simple theft he progressed to breaking into shops and houses, something relatively easy to do in wartime Glasgow, and was so able to finance his love of expensive clothes and fine dining, a pastime which allowed him to 'absorb the manners and behaviour of the rich and privileged'.

At one point, he decided to do 'his bit' for his country and applied to join the Merchant Navy, but after a week's training he was simply told he wasn't needed. He wrote:

> No explanation was given. I suspected that it was connected with the incident at Catterick and I had been labelled 'subversive'. They left me no option, I went back to burglary. If they wouldn't give me a suitable job, then I would create my own. I robbed houses all over the city.

He would later realise that if he became a butler he would easily be able to get close to his employer's valuables, but he still fondly recalled some of the successful scams and break-ins he had pulled off during his early career, such as stealing from Red Cross tins during the war and dressing up in expensive clothes to case rich properties under the guise of renting them for wealthy parents returning from India.

Indeed, after that last scheme, which netted him a small fortune, he reckoned he would have to lie low for a while to avoid police attention, so he took a job as a trainee receptionist at the Glenburn Hotel on the Isle of Bute. Once again he claimed that, due to 'secreting more pheromones than the average man', he had a constant stream of sexual partners, and as almost all of them gave him presents for his services, he clearly reckoned he was the Midnight Cowboy thirty years before the film was made!

According to 'Roy Fontaine', the first time he used this alias was in 1942 when he was dining alone in Glasgow's prestigious Central Hotel and a cultured Jewish gentleman asked him if he would dine with him. After dinner, the pair retired to his room where they had sex and Fontaine discovered his lover was the entertainer Vic Oliver. The relationship was to last and Fontaine described attending many wartime parties in Oliver's company, including one in the composer and singer Ivor Novello's flat in London's Piccadilly Circus, where the young men acted as waiters and the older men fondled them. Such events were said to be beautifully decadent but discretion was important as in those days the careers of many of the men involved would be ruined if they were outed. They purportedly included Lord Mountbatten, the playwright Terence Rattigan and the politician and journalist Beverley Baxter.

Looking back, Fontaine remembered that he felt as if he had 'died and gone to heaven' as he had arrived in a social sense and was accepted as a well-bred young gentleman by the elevated company he now moved amongst.

So, according to Roy Fontaine, by the age of eighteen he had come a long way from his humble roots, funded by scams and robberies, and was now rubbing shoulders with the great and the affluent. He was clearly ruthlessly ambitious and had become adept at using his good looks and charm on both sexes to get what he wanted. He had learned some valuable life lessons about people. Now it was time to start using them.

2

A FEEL FOR NOBILITY

At the end of the war, Fontaine took a flat in central London and as commuters streamed off to work in the city centre, he travelled to the suburbs and broke into their houses. Imprisonment soon followed and by the spring of 1952, when he was released from Wandsworth Prison after a two-year sentence for 'smash and grab' raids on two London jewellery shops, Fontaine reckoned he was ready for an in-service post. He had read about what was required of a butler and he had honed his knowledge of jewellery, porcelain and antiques in the prison library.

However, when he returned to his parents' house in Glasgow he immediately realised that their marriage was in trouble. Shortly after that, his mother left his father to become house-keeper in a castle in Dunblane, Perthshire, and when Fontaine visited her, he was asked by the then owner, Mrs Dunsmuir, to stay on to be the driver and odd-job man about the place. He noticed two things immediately – the many valuables on show and the Swedish maid, Agnetha.

One significant event Fontaine recalled from his time in Dunblane was the arrival of his prison friend, John Wootton. An invitation from Fontaine led to Wootton turning up one sunny day when both employer and staff were enjoying drinks on the lawn. That was to be Wootton's second meeting with Fontaine's mother, who now called herself 'Marion', and in due course, Wootton was to marry her and become Fontaine's stepfather.

However, Fontaine's foremost memory from Dunblane was

of the beautiful Agnetha. He again detailed their powerful attraction to one another, but unfortunately the relationship caused problems. Fontaine's employment finished abruptly one day when Mrs Dunsmuir unexpectedly entered a bedroom where Agnetha and Fontaine were having sex. Mrs Dunsmuir demanded he leave at once, but Fontaine, with admirable *sangfroid*, responded, 'Certainly, Madam. If you give me a cheque in lieu of a month's wages, I will be on my way.'

The employer reluctantly paid the money and Fontaine took off for a two-week holiday in Jersey with Agnetha, who had also decided to leave her job.

After that, Fontaine obtained new references 'for a price' then scoured the 'top people's' magazines looking for available posts. By that stage, he had decided that an in-service post was attractive on two fronts, namely living in comfortable surroundings whilst being able to assess what valuables were worth taking. On top of that, he had built up criminal contacts who were able to make convincing fake jewellery which he could swap for the real thing as most people were unable to tell the difference.

There was another reason though: 'I enjoyed nobility, it was something I had a feel for.'

Using his bogus references, Fontaine moved on to Park Hall, Drymen, Stirlingshire, owned by a family called the Warren-Connells. They were wealthy 'old money' and Fontaine worked hard to gain their trust, which was quickly earned. When the family went on holiday, he took over the various household duties, including opening all the mail in his employers' absence. One day, according to Fontaine, an invitation for Mr Warren-Connell arrived for the Queen's Garden Party at Edinburgh's Holyroodhouse. On reading it, it occurred to him that as he had already been 'a guest of Her Majesty on a number of occasions' – mainly in Barlinnie and Wandsworth and 'none of them enjoyable' – he owed it to himself to take his employer's place at the soiree.

Fontaine went on to explain how he accomplished such a deception. He allegedly hired a morning suit then drove the family's

Bentley to the royal residence in Edinburgh where a uniformed policeman checked his invitation, then saluted him and waved him through. As Fontaine mingled, he rubbed shoulders with top policemen and judges as they all enjoyed paper-thin cucumber sandwiches, completely unaware of who he really was.

He also described taking the opportunity to visit an acquaintance, wealthy shop owner Esta Henry, in nearby Mowbray House, presenting her with a dozen red roses and letting slip that he was on his way to 'The Garden Party'. She was most impressed and his credibility was now beyond reproach, thus softening her up for the raid he was planning on her shop.

His time at Park Hall was limited, though.

Two Stirlingshire CID men, aware of his background, paid him a visit and quizzed him about some recent local crimes. After he had answered all their questions, the pair drove off, seemingly content with what they had heard and even wishing him luck, but that night they phoned Park Hall to warn Warren-Connell about him. Fontaine happened to listen in to the call and when his employers summoned him and asked him about his criminal past, Fontaine knew it was better to tell the truth. Despite this revelation, the Warren-Connells supposedly offered him a second chance, but Fontaine felt unable to take it as he knew he would be the chief suspect for any future crimes in the area.

Fontaine then stated, however, that when he told them he was leaving, the Warren-Connells became very upset. They firstly tried to get him a post with friends of theirs and when he declined that, they insisted he have three months' salary instead, whereupon he left for London to stay with his mother and Wootton in the Paddington flat they were now sharing.

His story thus far paints a self-flattering picture of a wealthy elite that was easily overwhelmed by his charm, would-be victims to his cunning. He had successfully utilised his cultivated prowess, but as yet both Mrs Dunsmuir and the Warren-Connells had managed to slip through his criminal grasp. It wouldn't be long, however, before his acquired contacts in the world of the rich began to pay off.

3

THE MOWBRAY HOUSE JOB

On his visits to Esta Henry in Edinburgh's Royal Mile, Fontaine had noticed she kept her most expensive items in a black deed tin in an office at the rear of the shop. He outlined his plan to steal the deed tin to Wootton, who agreed they should go ahead with it.

Fontaine detailed their plot as follows: he would enter the shop and get talking to Mrs Henry and after a short time, Wootton would call the shop from a phone box outside. She would then most likely answer the call using the phone at the front of the shop, at which point Fontaine would sneak into the office at the rear of the premises carrying a briefcase containing three telephone directories. He would then empty the tin box into the briefcase and put the directories into the box to make up the lost weight and quickly leave, doffing his hat to Esta on the way out as a signal to Wootton that the raid had been successful. Wootton would then start the getaway car.

He wrote that, 'the plan that I had formulated was exactly how it happened. Esther smiled at me as I left.' He continued that the pair then drove south, Fontaine taking half the haul with him on a train from Carlisle to London and Wootton taking the other half with him in the car.

It was 1953 and they had reportedly just committed Scotland's biggest ever jewel robbery to the tune of £100,000. The cache consisted of American and Canadian dollars and jewels of every description. The heist had been so successfully executed that it was not discovered until the next day when Esta's son, Louis, had to call in a locksmith to open the tin – Fontaine having taken the keys with him – to then find out that the valuables were gone.

Knowing that he and Wootton would be suspects, they went to Torquay and, posing as rich American businessmen, booked into a first class hotel there. Their cover was apparently so good that one night the assembled company sang 'The Star Spangled Banner' in their honour and, in effect, they had Torquay 'in the palms of their hands' and could have passed as many dud cheques as they wanted, but in view of their recent enrichment, had no need to do so. Fontaine then paid Wootton a fair price for the remaining forty pieces of jewellery they still hadn't sold on – including some of the Hungarian Crown Jewels – and he left them in an old and trusted criminal contact's attic in London's East End.

He was able to do so because: 'Among the thieves I worked with, there was a code of honour. None of us would break it, it was our bond, our only security in a world of law-abiding grasses.'

Shortly after he had done that though, Fontaine was arrested near the house Wootton now shared with Marion in Margate and all three of them were transported overnight by train to Edinburgh. There on the platform to meet them, Fontaine claimed, was none other than the Chief Constable of the city. He approached and shook Fontaine's hand, saying, 'So you're Fontaine. Well, I'm glad it was one of her own – and not foreigners as the press have been speculating.'

When the case went to court, the prosecution offered them a deal which involved the true value of the stolen jewels not being made public; Fontaine was against doing any deal with the police, but as it involved Marion walking free and Wootton facing only a charge of receiving stolen property, he was persuaded to take it. According to Fontaine, Wootton got four years' imprisonment and Fontaine three, but crucially, the case against Marion was dropped.

Serving his time in Barlinnie Prison in Glasgow, Fontaine

realised he had taken a further 'step up the criminal ladder' as all the newspapers carried his and Wootton's pictures and described them as 'gentleman thieves'. He remembered how other inmates queued up to shake their hands and even the warders were well disposed towards them. Even more remarkably, Esta visited him in prison to try to find out where her missing jewels were, but to no avail.

Ever-willing to detail his sexual exploits, Fontaine described how he came to terms with his sentence, passing the time having a homosexual relationship with a prison warder and, on being transferred to a women's prison towards the end of his sentence, having sex with a female inmate.

When he was released in the winter of 1955, he reported going straight to Esta's shop, again taking her a bunch of red roses. When he entered, the shop cleaner berated him for betraying Esta's friendship; Esta, however, accepted the flowers with a smile. Apart from obviously wanting her jewels back, Fontaine wrote, 'The cleaning woman had it wrong. I hadn't betrayed my friendship with 'Esther', she had always been a "mark". She was wealthy and I was a thief, but we truly liked each other.'

He concluded his memories of the Mowbray House job with a description of his journey to London to retrieve the briefcase he had left in the friend's attic, stating that, 'The suitcase that I had left with him had never been opened. Honour.' These final remarks underline the importance he claimed he placed on loyalty. The ill-founded devotion to a criminal honour system pervades Fontaine's mental justification for his later crimes and hints at a more sinister willingness to pass judgement on those who did not adhere to his warped ethical code.

4

THE SHEIK STING AND THE FIANCÉE FIDDLE

After his release in 1955, Fontaine quickly returned to his old exploits, while also thinking up some brand new scams. One of his best ruses yet, he claimed, came in 1956 after a cultural foray in Paris.

According to Fontaine, he had hired a sheik's headdress from a theatrical costumier, iodined his skin to make it look darker and bought twelve good quality suitcases before phoning to book himself into a high-class hotel as 'Sheik Mutlak Medinah'. He then arranged for a chauffeur-driven Rolls-Royce to drop him off at the hotel and he checked in wearing full Arab gear. Once there, he bombarded the hotel switchboard with bogus calls supposedly from embassies, banks and stockbrokers. He stayed in his room for a few days, all the while tipping the staff generously.

He then asked the management to book him into another, better class hotel, reasoning that the staff at the second hotel would be reassured by the fact that the booking was made through the previous one. Growing into his role 'the way an actor does', he went through the same routine but this time arranged to be booked into the Dorchester, which was to be the scene of the sting.

He knew the famous hotel well and was aware that the suites had two exits. On his third day there, he called the manager and asked if he could see some of the jewellery for sale in the hotel shops. When it was delivered to his room, he feigned disappointment, so the manager called some jewellers from Hatton Gardens who sent their assistants to his suite with samples of their top-class merchandise.

Before long, Fontaine continued, the suite was filled with eager jewellers trying to tempt him with their wares, but he pointedly appeared disinterested before announcing that he would think about which items to buy whilst bathing. He then filled the bath with hot water, causing the room to become steam-filled and once that was done, extended an arm from the bathroom and asked to see the jewels again. After the eager assistants passed the gems through the bathroom door, Fontaine quickly disrobed and left through the other exit in the business suit he was wearing underneath his robes, having transferred all the jewels into his own briefcase.

Although the setup had cost him a few thousand pounds, it netted £300,000 and six worried jewellers eventually discovered six empty cases and some discarded robes in the bathroom. He recalled:

> My confidence was now sky high. If there was a better thief in Britain, I didn't know of him. For that matter, neither did the police. Talking of which, I was never questioned or charged with that job.

He also described studying rings in shop windows, then commissioning excellent copies so that when he pretended he was interested in buying a ring, he could deftly make the switch, leaving the unsuspecting jeweller with the copy. Again, the initial outlay was expensive, but the rewards were worthwhile.

A less sophisticated ruse involved going into a jeweller's shop with a 'fiancée'. The female accomplice would ask to see a certain ring that had taken her eye, and after she had it in her possession, Fontaine would ask if they could see it in daylight. Outside in the street, Fontaine would drop his cigarette lighter, knowing that the assistant would show 'true servile deference' by instantly bending down to pick it up for this potentially valuable customer.

At that point, Fontaine and his 'fiancée' took off to Wootton's waiting car and sped away.

Fontaine fondly remembered those 'halcyon days' when he was 'at his peak'. Unfortunately for him, they weren't to last long.

5

THE MONTAGUE ARMS AND HENLEY BREAK-INS

Fontaine was at this point living in Knightsbridge, where he rented a flat whilst plotting his upcoming schemes. One day, he claimed he was enjoying a brandy in an expensive lounge in Windsor when he got talking to an attractive young girl who accepted his invitation to join him for a drink. At first he thought he 'might fuck her' but when she started talking about a heavy drinking publican she once worked for in Slough, he began to listen and saw the prospect of some future business.

He plied her with drink and when she mentioned a safe in the pub's basement that was packed with large denomination notes and jewellery, he had heard all he wanted to hear and quickly left. He then flew to Edinburgh and recruited a safe blower called Ambrose Carr.

He and Carr then rented a flat near to the Montague Arms and became regulars there, meeting the likes of the broadcaster Gilbert Harding and his gay lover. Fontaine explained his professional philosophy as follows:

> They were wealthy well-connected men. These friendships, as with Esther Henry, were purely superficial. I was on the lookout for useful information. If I had sex, well, that was a bonus.

Fontaine relished the details of their devious and calculated plotting. He described how they carefully noted the publican's

16

daily routines and befriended the resident Great Dane by feeding it raw meat.

They made their move at 3am one morning when the landlord and his wife were blind drunk. When the dog appeared, Fontaine led it to a hut where he locked it in as it happily chewed on a bag of steak he had given it. Carr then blew the safe and they left with £29,000 in cash and some jewellery. Upon returning to their rented rooms, the pair showered and changed, disposing of the clothes they had been wearing so that police forensics would have nothing on them. Carr then left for home and Fontaine returned to London.

An impressive tale of a well-executed, professional piece of work.

Shortly after that, Fontaine was again wondering what his next job might be when he met a drunken *au pair* in a pub near Maidenhead. She told him that her rich employers had recently taken all their valuables out of their safety deposit box and hidden them in their house in Henley, and that they were shortly going to the United States on holiday. The girl also told him the address of the house, so the next day, Fontaine went to the front door and when no one answered, he broke in expecting to find the family treasure. However, after an attempt to locate the hidden valuables proved futile, Fontaine claimed to have instead stolen a Renaissance-period Spanish galleon encrusted with rubies and diamonds.

Surprisingly enough, Fontaine then proceeded to 'cheekily' offer the artefact to Esta Henry's son Louis in Edinburgh. Despite the stupidity of this risk, Fontaine was even so bold as to reject Louis' offer of £2,000 as being far too low. Louis must have then called the police, for shortly after that, Fontaine's hotel room was visited by five policemen – one of them being an old acquaintance: the Chief Constable of Edinburgh.

Although Fontaine was interrogated for four hours – in truth, he contended, all 'part of a professional's work' – he gave them nothing and they were forced to release him.

It annoyed him, though, that he had failed to find the family's jewels, so Fontaine brazenly returned to the house in Henley. This time, he successfully located the valuables, worth a few thousand pounds, and stashed them in his safety deposit box at Harrods for safekeeping.

His luck was about to change though. On 7 January 1956, police smashed in the door of his Knightsbridge flat and arrested him for three break-ins, including those at the Montague Arms and the Henley household. At Buckinghamshire Quarter Sessions, Fontaine was sentenced to ten years for each break-in and five years for possession of a revolver found in his flat, making a total of thirty-five years; but as the ten years for the break-ins ran concurrently, the actual sentence was only fifteen years. Nonetheless, he was resentful of this punishment and wrote:

> This was tantamount to a life sentence in Britain. I had been done for three robberies, all without violence, all against wealthy people who were well insured. This sentence was out of all proportion to the crimes. I got five years for a gun that had never been fired or used in intimidation. This left a bitter taste in my mouth. The man before me in the dock was a paedophile, convicted of sexually molesting fourteen young boys. He got six years. With time off, he would be hanging around school playgrounds in four. English justice makes me sick. It is designed to protect property more than people. It is implemented by the rich. A fucking pervert who wrecks children's lives is treated more leniently than a thief.

This, however, was only the beginning of his mounting hatred for the English penal system. He was increasingly convinced that his crimes against the rich were inherently justified, and hence his sentences were undeserved.

6

FROM INSIDE TO IN-SERVICE

After serving part of the 1956 sentence in Parkhurst Prison on the Isle of Wight, Fontaine was transferred to Nottingham following an attempted escape. The regime there was more relaxed and 'brought the best out of him', as illustrated when he gave his word to return to prison after being granted unescorted leave to attend his father's funeral in 1962. He had told the prison governor, 'My father was a law-abiding lay preacher. To be at his graveside hand-cuffed and under escort, would shame his memory.'

Of course, by the time of Archibald Hall senior's death, Marion had been living with Wootton for years. Apparently no longer concerned about shaming Archibald's memory, Fontaine and his mother went to his father's house after the funeral and, while Fontaine kept the solicitor busy, Marion took some 'keepsakes'. Fontaine then 'had his needs satisfied' with a woman friend before reluctantly returning to prison, vowing never to give his word to 'the enemy' again.

Despite having been sentenced to a total of fifteen years' preventive detention in 1956, Fontaine was given parole in 1963 thanks to a change in policy announced by the Home Secretary. On his release, he immediately phoned Harrods to give them his measurements for a new suit and Marion and Wootton hastily arranged a party to celebrate. They invited friends from all over the country and many criminals came long distances to attend. He noted, 'There was no doubt that, as far as criminals were concerned, I had a lot of respect. I was most definitely first division.'

The following week, he was best man at the wedding of his mother and Wootton, which was a great day for him, soured only by a guest he had done time with in Winchester Prison stealing Marion's wedding present money. When confronted by Fontaine, the guest denied it, but Fontaine told him to 'fuck off' and that 'you don't take from your own'.

After the initial excitement of release, Fontaine started to look for work again. This time though, he started looking through the pages of the society magazine *Tatler* for a butler's post, reasoning:

> I had always enjoyed being 'in-service'. Besides living in beautiful homes that I could rob, there was also the air of class. My appreciation for antiques, beautiful jewellery and culture are separate from my criminality. Working for the rich meant I could indulge both aspects of myself.

He was able to find work fairly quickly and took a post in Sussex where he met a woman called Phylis who was the live-in cook. They moved on as a couple and took resident posts with the diplomat Nigel Law in Chalfont St Peter. In the Laws' household Fontaine saw and admired true wealth. The Laws never dined alone and their conversation was 'sparkling with wit, the house ablaze with shimmering silver and gold', and he asserted: 'If I could have been born to their lifestyle, I would never have become a thief.'

But Fontaine had to make up for the disadvantages he believed life had dealt him, so upon noticing that certain items were not listed on the silver inventory, he stole them and sold them for £3,000. He also copied the keys to the safe, intending to use them after he had left the Laws' employment.

He and Phylis then moved on to work for Sir George and Lady Aylwen. Fontaine was particularly proud of the fact that they had submitted false references and when Lady Aylwen phoned the Laws to check them, Fontaine answered the call, successfully impersonating his employer and giving himself a glowing testimonial.

Fontaine next recounted how, shortly after starting at the Aylwens', he realised that the lady of the house was in the habit of having affairs with younger men whom she liked to control to the point of cruelty. He recalled experiencing her domineering side one night when she summoned him to her bedroom. She was sitting up in bed wearing a low-cut negligee, looking, he thought, much like Marlene Dietrich. She ordered him to find her cigarettes, which he did fairly easily, then left. She called him back though to look for her lighter, which was beside her, so he handed it to her and left again. When she called him back once more, this time to light her cigarette, he became angry, and having lit her cigarette, asked her if she wanted anything else. At that she unzipped his trousers, so he climbed into bed with her and they had sado-masochistic sex. He hid the marks of the encounter from Phylis, but they split up soon after and went their separate ways.

After the break with Phylis he became an employee of the very wealthy Sir Charles Clore, whom he found nervous and unpersonable. He surveyed Clore's fabulous wealth, intending to rob him 'for millions', and planned one big hit before fleeing abroad. However, he had not reckoned that Clore was completing an insurance proposal form which disclosed that he, Fontaine, was a new employee. This caused investigators to quickly discover his true identity, so he was asked to leave before he could carry out his plan.

In any event, he was arrested for two jewel robberies shortly after that and given ten years' preventive detention at London Quarter Sessions in January 1964. Yet despite these consequences, his experiences as a butler thus far had been useful to him. Fontaine had finally found a way to get close to true wealth. He had caught a glimpse of the life fate had denied him and was determined to use his experience on his release to take matters into his own hands yet again.

7

CRIME SPREE 1965

This time Fontaine was sent to Blundeston Prison in Suffolk. But it was not long before he broke out with two other prisoners, George Thomas Patrick O'Neill and Donald Whitaker. With help from friends, they fled to the Glasgow area using stolen cars. Fontaine was on the run for eight months until his recapture in May 1966 but rather than lying low in that time, he broke into various houses, stealing jewellery and other valuables. He was also given information from friends of friends. He summed it up thus:

> When you are a known villain, ordinary people love to give you information. It's as if they break the law by proxy. Associating with criminals seems to hold a fascination for some. They wouldn't want to do the crime, or the time, but they like to buy you drinks, possibly because they think you're on their side.

Accordingly, he got wind of a bookmaker who was in the habit of keeping large amounts of cash in his house, so he, O'Neill and Whitaker went to the man's door posing as policemen. They got in but when the man asked to see their search warrant, Fontaine calmly informed him that he didn't have one and that they were robbing him, and then apologised for doing so. Fontaine claimed that they each got a few thousand pounds from the job and that he even anonymously reported the man to the police when they found out he was a fence for stolen goods.

Fontaine went on to describe how, after O'Neill was recaptured by the police, he and Whitaker carried out a successful daylight smash and grab raid on a jeweller's shop in Falmouth, Cornwall. And then, after Whitaker was recaptured, Fontaine soldiered on alone.

He then met a young pregnant Irish girl called Margaret in a London hotel and they moved in together in a flat in Regent Street where they lived as a couple. Fontaine claimed that during this time, he contacted some old friends and they carried out a precision raid on 'Gerrards' the jewellers. This involved paying thousands of pounds to insiders at a security firm who arranged for the alarms to be switched off at a precise time to allow the thieves to scoop hundreds of thousands of pounds' worth of gems, after which the alarms were reactivated.

Knowing that the police would suspect only a select few of a raid of that magnitude, Fontaine and Margaret made for Eastbourne on England's south coast where he enjoyed reading about the raid. It seemed that Broadway star Beatrice Lillie and the Marchioness of Abergavenny were two of the owners of the stolen jewels, but Fontaine was not concerned; he had other things on his mind, explaining that, 'Putting to one side the sadness and loss of those I had robbed, I went out on the town with Margaret.' He continued:

> Margaret was well suited to me in that she loved the high life. We both adored the thrill of casino gambling, eating the best food and living life with a zest. Sex was good, her body was young and firm. She was passive and enthusiastic at the same time. I was her guide, her Svengali.

After Eastbourne, Fontaine recalled renting a farmhouse with Margaret in Kent where he carried out two well-planned stings.

Firstly he fleeced the landlady who had rented them the farmhouse by enticing her into a non-existent property deal, paying her regular dividends from her own capital before clearing out her bank account.

On the night they left the farmhouse for good, he arranged for the manager of the local jewellery shop to call round with some expensive items. He had built up a roaring fire and insisted on the unwitting salesman joining him in a Christmas Eve drink. In preparation for the final sting, he had placed bundles of cash round the room, but then paid using a worthless cheque. He and Margaret left that night for Wales, then moved on to Weston-super-Mare, where he was eventually arrested.

He later appeared at Edinburgh High Court in May 1966 and got five years for various charges of theft and fraud committed during his time on the run. It had been an astonishing period during which he had stolen a fortune, looked after a young girl who had fallen in love with him and acted as a father to the baby girl she had given birth to. Indeed, after Fontaine was sent back to prison, Margaret and her newborn baby Caroline stayed with the Woottons. When Margaret later went to Canada, she left baby Caroline in England and Fontaine referred to her as his 'daughter' from then on.

But he certainly wasn't to be the best of fathers, as he was now returning to an even lengthier stay in prison.

8

THE PARKHURST WARDER CASE

On top of his latest sentence, Fontaine still had to serve the sentence passed in England from which he had escaped. Accordingly, he was again sent to Parkhurst Prison on the Isle of Wight where the regime was brutal. He reasoned, 'If I became a murderer, then some of the officers there should hold their hands up and say: "We helped to shape him into what he was."'

A warder he encountered there 'embodied all that is worst about prison corruption'. Fontaine claimed that this warder charged hundreds of pounds to alter inmates' prison records so that the parole board would be presented with a cleaned-up version of a prisoner's behaviour in custody, making release more likely.

Fontaine 'did business' with the warder but quickly became disillusioned with his methods. He said the man had a sadistic nature and was in the habit of beating up prisoners for no obvious reason, so Fontaine and others got together and decided to expose him. The reasoning was as follows:

We decided to inform the Governor about him. To turn in someone who can bring your release date closer might seem strange, but hate and fear are powerful emotions. Our only weapon against him was his own corruption.

The third time Fontaine spoke to the governor about the warder, he was told his accusations were unfounded, so in frustration he produced copies of his own prison records and showed them to the governor. After that, Fontaine explained, the governor had to take him seriously and act on the obvious dishonesty before him. In due course, eleven other inmates were interviewed, which eventually led to the warder being arrested. The prison authorities tried to bribe inmates with offers of parole if they gave any information that could help the prison officer, but no one came forward as 'sadists don't elicit much sympathy'.

The atmosphere at Newport Magistrates' Court was electric as the prisoners told their stories and the warder was committed for trial at Winchester. The campaigning journalist Paul Foot wrote an article about prison corruption in *Private Eye* and prisoners brave enough to speak up against the regime at Parkhurst expressed fears of increased future brutality should the warder be acquitted and reinstated. The police officer in charge of the case, however, reassured the anxious inmates that the case was sound.

Then, just before the trial started, the judge and the prosecutor originally set to try the case were changed and the Prison Officers' Association paid for a top QC to defend their man. The main issue was that, as prison inmates did not have access to money, it would be impossible for them to pay the warder for the service he was allegedly offering. In any event, the defence argued, the whole thing was simply a plot hatched by a few high-profile inmates to try to ensure that they would be transferred out of Parkhurst to other jails with softer regimes. Fontaine observed:

> Anybody with any knowledge of prison life knows that this is rubbish. Money is used on the inside as much as it is on the outside. The only difference is that people on the outside put it in a wallet, and prisoners stick it up their arses.

Fontaine recalled that as he waited in the court building to give evidence at the trial, he spoke to the detective in charge of the case who told him that he thought the defence's 'money point' was ludicrous. On the way out of the room, however, the policeman dropped a £10 note that Fontaine quickly picked up before being called to give evidence. He later described what happened in the court:

> The defence counsel's inference that I was an inveterate liar was immensely irritating. After hearing my testimony being ridiculed yet again, I spoke once more. 'It seems that whatever I say, you are not prepared to give me the benefit of the doubt.' Reaching into my breast pocket, I produced the banknote. 'Perhaps, this will speak more eloquently than any words I might say.' I held the note up for the judge to see. I heard him say: 'Am I to understand that this is a Treasury note?' The clerk of the court came over to me and, taking it, gave it to the judge for closer inspection. If prisoners didn't have money, what the fuck was this? The court fell silent.

Despite the strength of the prosecution case, and much to Fontaine's disbelief, the warder was eventually acquitted. As a result, all the prisoners who had spoken up against him were transferred to Winchester Prison and systematically beaten up. In Fontaine's case, though, the warders went through the motions; having taken him to an empty cell and smashed up his few possessions, they stopped short of assaulting him and he was then moved to Hull Prison.

Embittered by this experience, he was to stay at Hull Prison until, according to his recollection, he was released on licence in 1970. His time at Hull, though, was marked by a happier occasion; it was there that Fontaine found true love.

With another male prisoner.

9

BARNARD

Fontaine first met the 'love of his life' Dave Barnard in Hull Prison in the late 1960s. Barnard had the cell next to Fontaine's and they immediately felt at ease in each other's company, something that was destined to develop into strong affection. They quickly fell into the habit of eating dinner together, having some wine and conversing in Fontaine's cell until lock-up.

As time went by, they realised their feelings 'went beyond the realms of ordinary friendship' and a sexual relationship developed. Fontaine declared that he felt 'more love for this human being than he had for any other'. He wrote: 'Just to be with him, just to look at him, made me feel whole . . . At the age of forty-six, I finally understood what it was to be in love.'

When Fontaine mated his canary with another inmate's, he gave the resultant chick to Barnard. He also transformed his cell 'into a place where a man could live with dignity', putting in a red bedspread, red curtains and a red carpet, as he thought red gave off warmth and hope.

Fontaine pondered his new situation:

Did Dave love me? Did I love him? Was this feeling real or would it vanish into the ether like a child's dream? I was given the answer when Dave argued with, and then threatened, a screw.

Fontaine felt that 'the core of his life had been taken from him' when Barnard was moved to the prison's punishment block and he then began to hate the prison officer involved. He admitted, 'There is a side of me, when aroused, that is cold and completely heartless. That uniformed bastard had crossed the line, he was on dangerously thin ice.' Accordingly, the next day Fontaine tried to scald the warder with hot tea, so he too was sent to the punishment block. He now knew for certain that he loved Barnard.

As for the future, he planned that he and Barnard might become 'legit' and open a restaurant or a club, and he realised he enjoyed thinking about a future that didn't involve being chased by the police. The jail's governor seemingly saw something of this change in his attitude and he recommended him for parole after Fontaine told him of his plans with Barnard. Fontaine recalled being released on licence in the winter of 1970, one of the conditions being that he was to spend eight months in a prison hostel in Preston. He took the offer with mixed feelings, as it meant leaving Barnard in prison:

> For Dave, it was truly awful. He loved me, he wanted me to be free, but he didn't want to lose me. In the end, his love proved to be unconditional – if I went, I could start to lay the bricks of our future.

His life of freedom was to be short-lived though, as his dreams of building a legitimate life proved impossible. When the opportunity arose, Fontaine leapt at the chance to take his crimes to an international level.

10

THE SOVIET CONSULATE AFFAIR

Upon his release from Hull Prison, Fontaine at first seemed dedicated to his professed desire to settle down with Barnard. However, after he started working in the kitchens of Whittingham Hospital, he met Mary Coggle, whom he slept with immediately after realising she was attracted to criminals. He then proceeded to use her as a go-between, having her carry messages and presents to Barnard since he was not allowed to visit the prison from which he had been released.

Claiming that he just needed someone to have sex with, he next bedded a local widow, Hazel Patterson. The Preston shop-owner, rightly or wrongly, came to regard herself as Fontaine's partner. She insisted on perfumed baths and lots of sex, but Fontaine recalled that he was really just going through the motions to keep her happy. He was still sleeping with Mary and had even added a young chef called Tony to his sexual conquests.

He eventually met Ruth Holmes, a woman who was introduced to him by an old prison friend called Rafferty. Declaring that Ruth was the only woman he ever loved – a fact that he easily reconciled with his continuing but inhibited relationship with Barnard – he eventually married her in September 1972. Despite the asserted 'purity' of their love, Ruth knew nothing of his previous lovers and believed that Fontaine was simply a 'slightly unscrupulous businessman'.

Shortly after their wedding, Fontaine was relaxing with Ruth at her London flat when he received a call from a 'completely

30

immoral' male friend who told him he had spent the night with a wealthy married man whose family were away on holiday. As he left the man's house the following morning, he had noticed a large leather briefcase on the hall table and, thinking it might contain something important, had picked it up on the way out.

The caller had apparently phoned Fontaine because he had been unable to spring the large combination lock on the brief-case and thought Fontaine might be interested in taking it off his hands. Fontaine agreed and went to meet the man, prom-ising him a 'fair price' if the contents were valuable. Back at Ruth's, he managed to open it and was astonished to find that it contained confidential cabinet papers and it occurred to him that it would be very embarrassing to the government should they be leaked.

Ruth, however, was upset and wanted Fontaine to burn them, but he already had other ideas. Although he had married Ruth, Fontaine was still in love with Dave Barnard. As Barnard was still in prison, Fontaine wondered if he would be able to barter the stolen papers for his freedom and so decided to secretly hold on to them without his wife's knowledge.

The next day he copied them and sent a copy to Wootton, after which he phoned the office of a cabinet minister to broach the deal. When he got as far as asking whether a serving pris-oner might be released in exchange for the stolen papers, it suddenly occurred to him that the authorities would easily be able to trace him if he named the prisoner, his relationship with Barnard being well known in Hull Prison.

Fearing a phone trace, he quickly hung up and gathered his thoughts:

I wanted the man I loved free. After some thought, it was clear that there was no way I could give them Dave's name, without leading them straight to me. I decided to see what the Russians would offer.

He went to the Soviet Consulate and told an official that he 'felt a friendship' with the Russian people and would like her to see the documents he had in his possession. He was passed on to another official who interviewed him and asked if his motive was money, which Fontaine denied. He was then asked if he would like to visit the Soviet Union and he said he would like to see the Bolshoi Ballet, the Fabergé collection and St Petersburg. The interview concluded when he was told that all of that would be possible, but in the meantime he was advised not to come back to the consulate as British intelligence was photographing everyone entering and leaving the building.

According to Fontaine, his next meeting took place in Hyde Park the following day. His contact said he was interested in seeing all of the papers he had, so he gave Fontaine his ex-directory number which Fontaine scribbled down on the back of a complimentary book of matches he had picked up from the Dorchester Hotel.

Fontaine then hid the briefcase and papers along with a gun and ammunition he had in the wine cellar of Grimshaw Hall in Warwickshire, where he worked as a butler. Shortly after that, he met up with Rafferty to discuss some stolen foreign currency he had. The pair agreed a price and the conversation moved on to other matters, including Barnard. As they talked, Fontaine let his emotions get the better of him and he confided in Rafferty what he had been doing to try to get Barnard released.

Rafferty, however, betrayed him, not only to the police, but also to Ruth. Fontaine realised what had happened when he next met his wife, the atmosphere being understandably frosty. He briefly thought about telling her lies, but decided not to, reasoning, 'How could I deny a relationship that was based on something so beautiful as selfless love?'

Given that logic, Ruth broke down in tears and Fontaine was left to curse the 'fickle finger of fate' which caused him to live a loveless life for forty-five years, then fall in love with two people within the space of eighteen months.

To make matters worse, Special Branch then came to Grimshaw Hall and recovered the briefcase and gun.

In custody once more, Fontaine's legal adviser told him to expect a jail sentence of between ten and fifteen years for breaching the Official Secrets Act. Despite that, Fontaine never once cracked to reveal who had actually stolen the briefcase.

Instead, Fontaine chose to fight his corner and instructed his lawyer to 'let them know that if they fucked him, he would fuck them'. He threatened to give the press details of all the prominent men in government who were using rent boys. The authorities took the deal and within a week – and in a closed court – Fontaine pleaded guilty to simple possession of the stolen briefcase and the gun and was sentenced to an astonishingly light two years inside. Still, the timing was poor for him, as it was then September 1973, just months before Barnard was due for parole.

Commander Wilson of Special Branch later came to see Fontaine in Wandsworth Prison and there mentioned 'the Russians' for the first time. As Wilson talked, he spread photographs of Fontaine's Soviet contacts on the table then showed him a photograph of the book of matches that had the contact number on it. It dawned on Fontaine that further prevarication was pointless, and he confessed:

> Also, as a lifelong professional thief and lover of the high life, the communist system is not one that is close to my heart. I'm closer to being a monarchist than a socialist. I gave him everything I could. He shook my hand when he left.

Commander Wilson had also hinted that Fontaine would not serve the full two-year sentence. That turned out to be true, and on top of that, he was sent to Long Lartin Prison in Worcestershire where Ruth visited him to try to sort out their problems. Fontaine told her that whilst he still loved her as much as he could any woman, he could not love her as much as he could a man and when he advised her to divorce him, she left the prison in tears.

However, this was not the end of Fontaine's romantic entanglements. He first met David Wright when they were in Long Lartin Prison together. According to Fontaine, Wright came into his cell to ask him about jewellery and they ended up having sex. Fontaine was not emotionally involved – as he was with Barnard – but even so, he admitted, 'once I had tasted him, I couldn't keep my hands off him'.

It wasn't long, though, before Barnard was paroled and Fontaine arranged for Mary Coggle to be at the gates of Hull prison to present Barnard with a Jaguar Hazel Patterson had given him. During the following few weeks, Barnard visited Fontaine regularly as they discussed their future plans together. But tragedy was soon to strike. Having been in prison for twelve years, Barnard was killed when he lost control of the car near Carlisle on the M6 in the spring of 1974. He had been at liberty for four weeks.

Fontaine's life had changed forever. He wrote:

This was a blow from which I would never truly recover. The tragic events that were to follow, the killing of innocent people, being condemned to live out the rest of my natural life behind bars, none of that would have come to pass if that high-powered car had reached its destination. It seemed to me that I had paid a terrible price for my wrongdoings. The anger and despair that I felt from having the only real love I had ever known snatched from me, would leave me less than human. What did I care for life now? My life, any life?

Obviously the scene was now set and the loss of Barnard, he claimed, pushed him over the edge. Whether or not Fontaine was always capable of murder or it was, as he said, the emotional scarring of Barnard's death that unleashed the killer, Fontaine was soon to become the true monster the world would remember him as.

11

LADY HUDSON AND THE MURDER OF DAVID WRIGHT

Despite Barnard's death, Fontaine carried on seeing Wright, the trade-off being that the 'thief of some standing and experience' allowed the younger man to pick his brains in exchange for his youthful body.

As Wright was being paroled before him, Fontaine told him all about the layout and security at Grimshaw Hall, where he had been a butler during his last bout of freedom. They made an agreement that Wright would pay him a percentage of the proceeds of the break-in. Afterwards, though, nothing came Fontaine's way. He was furious: 'As time went by, no word. I had bought him clothes, set up a job for him, and nothing. Lowlife! He was just a whore.'

Then, in 1977, Fontaine was leafing through the pages of *Country Life* when he noticed a butler's post being offered by Lady Margaret Hudson at Kirtleton in Dumfriesshire. Lady Hudson was the widow of MP Sir Austin Hudson who died in 1956. She was a Justice of the Peace in Dumfriesshire and ran the historic Kirtleton Estate near Waterbeck in Dumfries and Galloway. She was small, in her early seventies and, apart from her occasional companion Mrs Lloyd, she was on her own – the perfect target for Fontaine. He applied for the post and before long he found himself working in a house packed with antiques that were worth a fortune. He recalled, 'Obviously I would rob her, but for the moment I was happy just to stay there.'

He was good at his job and Lady Hudson was 'well taken'

with him. Each day Fontaine inspected her jewellery, his intention being eventually to steal it, but only after he had left Lady Hudson's employment.

However, the appearance, and subsequent murder, of David Wright at Kirtleton changed things. Shortly after taking the post, Fontaine had heard from Wootton that Wright was trying to contact him, so he got in touch with Wright and arranged to meet him at Carlisle Station.

Lady Hudson gave Wright odd jobs to do, so the two men were able to spend time together. During this time, Wright told Fontaine that he was wanted for the murder of a man in a gents' toilet and was happy to hide away for a while. Fontaine, of course, spent much of his time coveting his employer's jewels, but Wright became increasingly impatient about when they were going to 'make their move'. Tensions arose and Wright dropped hints about telling Lady Hudson about Fontaine's past if he continued to refuse to steal the jewels. Wright also ran up large gambling debts with local bookies, which Fontaine had to take care of. He wrote, 'He was an ungrateful little bastard. Yet still I let him stay.'

Fontaine's patience was wearing thin, though, and matters came to a head when Wright stole one of Lady Hudson's diamond rings. As soon as Fontaine noticed it was gone, he searched Wright's room and found it rolled up in one of his socks. When Wright appeared later, the pair argued and then Wright angrily drove off to the local village.

By that time, Fontaine explained, a pattern had developed. They would argue about when it was right to steal the jewels, then Wright would go out and get drunk, come home, apologise, then they would have sex and it would be forgotten about until the next time.

This night, however, Wright reappeared in Fontaine's room with a gun. He fired a shot at him that went through the bed's headboard, causing Fontaine to sit up in time to see an intoxicated Wright staggering towards him. Fontaine later recalled:

In the doorway stood a drunken Wright, in his hand the smoking weapon. Drunkenly he walked towards me. He started screaming: 'We're not gonna work here anymore. We're gonna rob it tonight.' I spoke calmly and quietly: 'Of course, Dave. We will. But let's leave it till the morning.' I feared for my life.

Fontaine tried to wrestle the gun from him but Wright struck him with it, bringing the butt hard against Fontaine's face. He was reduced to pleading for his life and agreeing to Wright's demands, but at that point Wright's anger turned to self-pity and he sank to his knees and started crying, saying he had had too much to drink. Fontaine took the gun from him, locked it away, then helped Wright to his room.

At that stage, as Wright had tried to shoot him, Fontaine had made his decision: 'I had decided to kill him. Tomorrow. I fucked him until I came, and then went back to my own room.'

According to Fontaine, he next phoned Wootton and told him what had happened. Wootton initially tried to dissuade him from killing Wright, but when he saw Fontaine had made his mind up, he then offered to help. However, as his oldest and dearest friend, Fontaine could not allow Wootton to become involved.

When Wright appeared for breakfast, he was 'shamefaced and contrite' but Fontaine reassured him that the previous night's events were forgotten about. He then invited Wright to go shooting with him and Wootton, who had arrived that morning, and Wright agreed. Wright selected a gun and eight cartridges, Fontaine took the gun Wright had tried to kill him with the night before and, along with Wootton and Tessa the Labrador, they set off for the moors. Fontaine wrote:

Each shot Dave took, I counted. When his eighth cartridge was spent, I spoke. 'Is your gun empty?' He smiled and said 'Yes'. I said: 'Are you sure? I don't want you trying to kill me again.' He thought I was jokily chiding him.

He gave me a rather coy expression: 'Roy, I've explained I was drunk and upset.' 'No, Dave. You tried to kill me last night.'

When Fontaine told Wright *he* was now going to kill *him*, he saw the same fear in Wright's face as he had experienced the night before. His anger rising, Fontaine carefully explained to Wright why he was about to kill him:

'You robbed me of my percentage in Grimshaw Hall, you sponge money off me, I pay your debts. When I tell you not to steal anything just yet, you take a diamond ring. I'm sick of your snide little comments about how her ladyship might discover my past. You try to blackmail me, and then you get drunk and try to kill me. Well, look where your pretty little face has got you now. You've ended up on the Scottish moors, and this is where you're going to die. The only use you ever had was to be fucked.'

Fontaine then shot Wright in the head and chest, before continuing:

'See! See, what you've made me do. You stupid, stupid greedy bastard.' I shot him again. His eyes were still open. 'It's alright for you, your troubles are over, mine are just beginning.' He made me rage, I shot him again.

He then ordered Wootton to leave before dragging the body into nearby bushes. He went back to the house to get a fork and spade, but when he returned and tried to break the ground up, he found it was so frozen that he thought that he might need a pneumatic drill to make an impression. Instead, he laid the body in a stream and placed earth and boulders over it until it was covered up, then he went home again, finding killing 'very stressful, very tiring'. In the course of the next week or so, he returned to the grave and placed more and more foliage on it, all the time cursing Wright for his greed and for making him do what he had done.

Wootton visited again the next weekend, so he and Fontaine went back to the murder site with a good bottle of Hock. Fontaine challenged Wootton to tell him where the body was hidden, but he was unable to. When he told him it was within three feet of where they were enjoying their wine, Wootton put his arm round him and congratulated him on committing the perfect murder.

As Lady Hudson had employed Wright as an odd-job man, Fontaine had to come up with a cover story for his disappearance. He told her that Wright had suddenly taken up the offer of a job in Devon and had asked him to pass on his thanks for her hospitality.

Just after that, however, Fontaine was listening in to his employer's telephone calls when he recognised the caller's voice. It was Hazel Patterson from Preston and she was saying that Her Ladyship's butler was a jewel thief who had served time; half an hour later the local police arrived and escorted him from the estate. He was taken to Gretna, where he checked into a hotel and Wootton arrived the next day to take him to Lytham. Lady Hudson had been sorry to lose him; not only had she paid him three months' salary, but she declared on record that she would never say Fontaine was anything other than a fine butler.

After the killing, Fontaine reckoned he had undergone a personality change, feeling a distance between him and the rest of the world and a coldness towards almost everything and everyone he encountered. He advised, 'I would say to someone who is thinking of killing: "Don't. Whatever it is that's released, you don't want set free."'

Fontaine was now a 'changed' man. He had experienced how murder could satisfy his thirst for vengeance against those who disappointed him. And once he had ventured into this level of criminality there was no turning back. Luck, in the form of a phone call, had saved Lady Hudson from the hands of the Monster Butler. Fontaine's next employers would not be so fortunate.

12

THE MURDER OF DOROTHY SCOTT-ELLIOT

After his expulsion from Kirtleton, Fontaine spent some time in Paris and London seeking anonymity before renting Middle Farm Cottage in Newton Arlosh near Carlisle for six months. He explained that he needed a place of sanctuary to collect his thoughts and told locals there that he was a recently divorced writer who wanted solitude. At times he contemplated ending it all by taking some pills, but his 'instinct to survive' prevailed and he decided instead to return to the more vibrant life of London.

Accordingly, he took a post as butler to the Scott-Elliots, a very wealthy couple who lived in Richmond Court, Chelsea. It was the autumn of 1977, and Fontaine described Walter Scott-Elliot as a frail, well-educated gentleman of eighty-two who had formerly been a Labour MP. His wife was twenty years his junior, was Anglo-Indian and irritable with the domestic staff, but despite that, she took a liking to Fontaine due, he thought, to him being a male who was fastidious in his nature and work. Their relationship developed into a 'friendship that went well beyond that of employer and employee'. When they were out together, Mrs Scott-Elliot introduced him as 'her friend Roy' and never as 'her butler'.

His plan was to empty the Scott-Elliot bank accounts and head off to sunshine and retirement. To begin with, he had his eye on a nearby flat that was accessible from the Scott-Elliots' flat for someone agile enough to climb over the roof and get in through the window. He told Mary Coggle, the woman he had met in Whittingham Hospital, of his plan and she recommended a friend of hers. He wrote, 'Two days later, I shook the hand of Michael Kitto – the worst day's work I have ever done.'

Having recruited Kitto to break into the neighbouring flat, Fontaine met up with him in the King's Cross pub where Mary Coggle worked. He recalled Kitto being so fascinated by his dazzling life of crime, as well as his knowledge of antiques and jewels, that by the end of the evening, Kitto asked if he could see round the Scott-Elliot flat. As Mrs Scott-Elliot was away at a private clinic that night and Mr Scott-Elliot was drugged up with sleeping pills, Fontaine saw no harm in letting Kitto see what genuine wealth was like. As they wandered around, Fontaine outlined his plans for stealing all of it in due course, and thought:

> For his part, he had never worked with a thief of my stature or experience before. I could tell that he would like to be my partner, would like to impress me. Maybe that was the motivation behind the action that changed both our lives.

Just as they were about to enter Mrs Scott-Elliot's bedroom, she unexpectedly opened the door and demanded to know what Kitto was doing there at that late hour. According to Fontaine, before he could answer, Kitto sprang at her and clamped his hands round her face, cutting off her air supply and causing her to slump to the floor, dead.

Fontaine had to think quickly. Not only was he seeing his 'island in the sun' disappearing fast, but he knew any enquiry into what had just taken place would uncover the thefts from the old couple that had already occurred, together with the break-in at the nearby flat. So he wrapped his 'old friend' in a silk bedspread and called Wootton, who immediately drove south to Chelsea.

The next day, Fontaine told Mr Scott-Elliot that his wife had gone to visit friends and that she had wanted him to dine at his club, which pleased the old man. Fontaine and Kitto decided to clear out as much as they could from the couple's accounts and they reckoned they only had a few days in which to do it. Fontaine and Mary, now decked out in Mrs Scott-Elliot's clothes and wig, went round various banks withdrawing cash, Fontaine forging the signatures since Mary was barely literate.

When Mr Scott-Elliot returned from the club that evening, Fontaine served the old man his usual whisky, which contained a crushed sleeping pill that would keep him in a confused state. Telling him that they had to go to meet his wife, who had now decided to visit friends in Scotland, they all drove north in Wootton's car. Kitto did the driving and Scott-Elliot sat between Fontaine and Mary, whom he introduced as one of his friends. He recalled the old man staring at her and obviously being unable to conjure up rational thought, but, 'This was just as well, because inches behind him, separated only by the moulded metal of the car boot, lay the body of his dead wife.'

They all stayed over at the cottage in Newton Arlosh that night and in the morning Fontaine and Wootton went into nearby Carlisle and hired a car. They transferred the body into the hired car's boot, put a spade and fork beside it and then Fontaine told Wootton to go home before the rest of them headed off to the Scottish Highlands.

On the way north, they stopped for lunch in Perthshire before travelling on to just outside the village of Braco. There, with the old man sound asleep, Fontaine and Kitto carried the body from the car boot to a shallow grave dug in a nearby field, then covered it with fern and heather. He recalled, 'Now that we were rid of her, the sense of relief was enormous. We drove back to Newton Arlosh, put the old man to bed and talked.'

Relieved as they may have been, they still had a major problem on their hands. They had murdered a woman and kidnapped her husband. Despite Walter Scott-Elliot being kept sufficiently docile with drugs, it was only a matter of time before he started to realise something was not quite right.

13

THE THIRD VICTIM –
WALTER TRAVERS SCOTT-ELLIOT

They had to decide what to do with Walter Scott-Elliot.

Time was needed to forge letters to stockbrokers and banks, empty worldwide accounts, and sell off the antiques and valuables from the Scott-Elliot home, but if they released the old man, his relatives would naturally be inquisitive about the whereabouts of his wife. On top of that, free of drugged drinks, Scott-Elliot would soon come back to his senses. Fontaine wrote, 'Old or not, he was still a man of some intellect. We decided to kill him.'

The decision had been made, so the next day they again drove north, this time to Blair Atholl in Perthshire where they stayed the night in the best rooms the Tilt Hotel could offer. As the others ate in the dining room, Scott-Elliot was made to eat alone in his room and in the morning they breakfasted with the man 'they were soon to murder'. After Scott-Elliot paid the bill by cheque, they continued north, the old man's captors looking for likely spots to carry out the deed.

When Scott-Elliot woke up and asked if they could stop so he could relieve himself, Fontaine watched as he went to the cover of some trees, then he signalled Kitto to get out of the car. Together they went into the woods after the old man. As Scott-Elliot was urinating, Fontaine caught hold of the old man's scarf and tried to strangle him. He was surprised at Scott-Elliot's strength and when he fought back and managed to get his hands under the scarf and keep his airways clear, Fontaine wrestled him to the ground. He then 'barked' at Kitto to get the spade from the car boot and hit him with it. Fontaine described the grisly scene:

> The spade crashed down on to the old man's skull, killing him. We dug a shallow grave within a copse of trees, and buried his thin, frail body. I remember saying: 'He put up more of a fight than I thought. He must have drawn strength from his noble Scottish ancestry.'

Afterwards, Fontaine, Kitto and Mary drove to Aviemore where they spent a few days. Whilst the other two drank heavily, Fontaine became withdrawn, running the recent events over in his head. He concluded: 'If I hadn't loved having sex with men, David Wright would still be alive. I truly believed that if I hadn't killed him, I wouldn't have killed anyone.' But despite Fontaine's soul-searching, he was by then a serial killer, and another murder was looming as Mary Coggle began to try Fontaine's patience.

14

MARY COGGLE'S MURDER

In Aviemore, Fontaine noticed that Mary was drinking too much and that she was drawing attention to herself. He was also concerned when she told him she had been making calls to friends in the King's Cross area of London, boasting of the high life she was now living. Fontaine became angry with her and tried to get her to see the danger they were all in if she carried on like that.

They returned to the cottage at Newton Arlosh, where Mary remained while Fontaine and Kitto went to London to clear the Scott-Elliot flat of antiques. When they returned, he found out that she had again been 'swanning around' the village wearing Mrs Scott-Elliot's fur coat and she had also been making more calls to her friends in London.

Fontaine realised she had become an embarrassment and he told Kitto that he was determined not to go to jail for life for the sake of a 'cheap prostitute' like her. According to Fontaine, he and Kitto discussed killing her, but he decided to talk to Mary first to see if she could adopt a lower profile. But then, 'Before we finished our conversation, Kitto said. "If she's awkward, I'll just fuck her one more time and then kill her."'

Fontaine spoke to her and she appeared to change her mind about keeping the fur coat, so he told Kitto he was free to fuck her but didn't have to kill her. The two men then set off to continue clearing the flat in London, but on their return, they discovered she had still been parading about wearing the fur coat. She said she had changed her mind and now wanted to

45

keep it after all. Mary's obstinancy thus sealing her fate, Fontaine left Kitto to do what he had to do.

He later recalled how that night, Mary and Kitto were drinking and they retired to the bedroom together. At about 3am, Fontaine claimed he was sitting alone in the living room when Mary appeared wearing only the fur coat and a pair of high heels. She asked him if he had ever made love on a fur coat before, then she spread it on the floor and lay on top of it. They had sex several times before she left to take a shower. Kitto then appeared in the living room and asked Fontaine if they should kill her; Fontaine was puzzled. He couldn't understand why Kitto hadn't killed her already. He recalled, 'It didn't surprise me that he hadn't. He was a weak character – weak, lazy and greedy.'

When Mary emerged again, Fontaine made to burn the coat in the roaring coal fire. When she protested, Fontaine smashed the poker over her head as Kitto pinned her arms together. The wig she was still wearing cushioned the blow and she was only knocked out, so Fontaine tied a plastic bag over her head and he and Kitto sipped brandy as she slowly suffocated. Fontaine reflected:

> Ten minutes later, I checked for her pulse. She was dead. Mary, my old friend, whom I had known for almost ten years. I regretted having to kill her. Before this I'd always liked her, she had a heart of gold, did Mary.

The two men then dressed the body in male clothes and tied a tie around her wrist, hoping it would look like a lesbian murder. They put the body in the boot of the car, waited until early morning, then drove across the Scottish border. Fontaine reasoned:

> I considered burying her near Dave Wright's body – fitting really, two prostitutes together. I dismissed the idea because, this close to Christmas, the Forestry Commission would be out on patrol, watching for tree thieves.

They eventually dumped the body near the village of Middlebie by throwing her over a hedge and into a stream.

Fontaine and Kitto then returned to London and briefly lived in the Scott-Elliot flat as they continued to clear it of its valuable contents. Fontaine explained that they had two differing aims in life – Kitto to become a successful criminal and Fontaine simply to take the money then fly off to his place in the sun.

But one more had to die before that.

15

THE FINAL MURDER – DONALD HALL

Fontaine's plan to get rich and then fly off to somewhere in the sun – probably in South America – was foiled by the release of his brother Donald from a three-year prison sentence. On leaving prison, Donald went to the house in Lytham that Wootton had shared with Marion before her death in 1975, but Wootton was not happy about Donald being there. He called Fontaine at the Scott-Elliots' flat and Fontaine assured Wootton that he would 'not let Don stay there and fuck up Wootton's life'. He told Wootton that Donald would have to go, admitting, 'My first thoughts were now of murder. It was becoming the easy solution.'

Fontaine initially thought he should drown his brother in the Irish Sea, but instead settled for drowning him in the bath at the cottage at Newton Arlosh. Donald disgusted him, as he thought his half-brother was a perverted child molester. Fontaine described him as follows:

Dirt under his fingernails, unshaven, slovenly, I hated having my half-brother near me. He filled me with contempt. He was scum, lowlife scum. The skinny child of a minuscule Army major. We didn't even have the same father, and he had none of my mother's characteristics or nature. Lowlife, nonce, ponce, scum, I was going to kill him. I would wait for the right opportunity.

That opportunity came on the very first night he was with

Donald, who spent the evening pestering Fontaine and Kitto about how much money they had. He was obviously keen to join the team and was out to impress them. When he offered to demonstrate how it was possible to tie someone up using only six inches of string, Fontaine obliged him by getting some string from the kitchen, which Donald then cut into two lengths of three inches. He then took his shoes and socks off, lay face down on the floor, folded his legs back and asked Fontaine to tie his big toes together. Donald then looped his hands over his feet and asked Fontaine to tie his thumbs together.

Donald seemed pleased with the demonstration, thinking it would enhance his image and prove his criminal ability, but Fontaine and Kitto were quick to take advantage of the situation. Fontaine went to the bathroom to soak a cotton-wool pad with chloroform while the unsuspecting Donald asked Kitto to untie him. When Fontaine returned, he and Kitto knelt down on either side of Donald, Kitto holding him down while Fontaine suffocated him with the chloroformed pad.

They then put the body in a hot bath to fend off rigor mortis and, 'to make sure he was clean', held him under the surface for about five minutes, which kept the body warm until it was time for it to go into the car boot.

With another seemingly perfect murder under his belt, Fontaine must have felt his days in the sun growing nearer. But with the body count now up to five, the stakes were also growing higher. All it would take was one minor slip-up to bring his proposed jet-setting future to a screeching halt.

16

THE LAST STOP

The next day they drove north-east, looking for a place to bury the body. It was January 1978 and heavy snow started falling which Fontaine thought might help cover the grave they were about to dig. Fontaine was cavalier about their situation, for 'having dead bodies in the boot of our car was no big deal. This was the third one in a matter of weeks.' The two men stopped in Dunbar to enjoy some warming drinks before carrying on to North Berwick. But the driving conditions grew treacherous as the snow began falling more heavily, so, fearing the consequences of an accident, they decided to stop somewhere for the night and postpone the burial till the next day.

In an ill-fated decision, they chose to rest at the Blenheim Arms Hotel. Fontaine recalled with malice:

> I was later to learn the name of the manager, Norman Wright. I wished I had never set eyes on him. He was one of those people who is suspicious by nature. If he saw children playing in the car park, he thought they were potential car thieves. He was fussy, and he proved to be my downfall.

According to Fontaine, Kitto was supposed to get false number plates for their hired car, mainly so they could keep it without paying for its hire, but there was another reason. The original number ended in 999 and being superstitious, Fontaine had no wish to bring bad luck on himself. He had advised Kitto to copy the registration number from a red Ford Granada the same year as the one they were driving, and to find out the owner's name so they could answer any questions if the police stopped them. He also told him to alter the tax disc to coincide with the new registration number.

However, Fontaine was soon to learn that Kitto had only told him he'd done as requested, while actually using random numbers on the plate and not bothering with the tax disc. As Fontaine angrily reflected, 'His stupid actions would lose us our liberty, forever.'

Not liking the look of them, Wright had phoned the police who immediately noticed the discrepancy between disc and plates. The police took Fontaine and Kitto to the police station, one of the officers driving the hired car with the dead body in the boot. Once there, Fontaine was allowed to use the toilet twice and he took the opportunity to flush away all the incriminating documents he had in his possession relating to the Scott-Elliots. On the second visit, Fontaine climbed out of the toilet window and hired a local taxi to take him to Dunbar, telling the driver his wife was in hospital there. Once there, though, he claimed she had been taken to Edinburgh and he had to go there, and the driver agreed to the fare. Fontaine believed that if he could get to Edinburgh, he could pick up some funds and then flee the country.

But shortly after that, the taxi was stopped at a police roadblock and Fontaine was taken to Musselburgh police station where he was asked about the body in the boot. Put in a cell, he asked for a drink of water then took an overdose of the barbiturates he had hidden rectally. After his suicide attempt failed, he awoke in hospital to face hours of questioning, and although he was 'vaguer than a wisp of smoke', it was to no avail as Kitto was telling the police all they needed to know.

17

FREEDOM'S END

Thanks to Kitto's confessions, the police soon learned of the cottage at Newton Arlosh and were able to match Mary's fingerprints to the body found at Middlebie. A pathologist from Edinburgh University had also discovered that Donald hadn't actually drowned but had been chloroformed to death. Despite this revelation, Fontaine still took pleasure in noting, 'It may have been a waste of time, but I had enjoyed holding him down!'

Because the police now seemed to know everything, Fontaine decided to assist them in finding the bodies. On 18 January 1978, he took them to the remains of Walter Scott-Elliot in Inverness-shire and on 21 January he took them to David Wright's body in Dumfriesshire. After that, they took two days to find Mrs Scott-Elliot's body in Perthshire.

When prosecuted, Fontaine was given two life sentences for the murders of David Wright and Walter Scott-Elliot but, having pleaded not guilty to the murder of Mrs Scott-Elliot, the court ordered that the 'file on that one remain open'. Kitto also received two life sentences at that hearing, Fontaine recalled.

Later that year they were transferred to the Old Bailey to face the murder charges relating to Mary and Donald, but by that time, Kitto was becoming anxious about how many life sentences he was going to end up with, so he started to talk again. Fontaine wrote, 'In an effort to get his sentence cut, he implicated John Wootton. I wanted him dead. A friend, a fellow con offered to help me out.'

Knowing that pure nicotine is poisonous, Fontaine arranged

for some to be slipped into Kitto's food. The plan was foiled when Kitto asked the warders to check it, but nobody knew who was responsible. Fontaine reasoned, 'If you're a prisoner and you grass, you should expect little else. I never touched him, but other cons poured scalding cocoa over his head.'

Kitto's lawyers tried to place all blame on Fontaine, claiming that he had dominated their client. Fontaine claimed this was rubbish as Kitto had had many opportunities to leave; the simple truth was that he was weak, and if anything, the whole episode was actually Kitto's fault as he had started it by killing Mrs Scott-Elliot. Fontaine maintained his innocence: he wanted to leave the Scott-Elliots 'skint but alive' and it all went wrong when he showed Kitto round the flat in Chelsea.

Serving his life sentence in Hull Prison, Fontaine complained that the 'screws' amused themselves by having fun at his expense. They knew he hated filth and squalor and that he continually cleaned his cell until it was to his liking, so they waited until he had scrubbed it up to his own standards then moved him to another filthy cell. After that happened repeatedly, and they stopped him getting his *Daily Telegraph*, he officially requested a move to a Scottish jail. He also started a hunger strike, his weight dropping from thirteen to five stones. Well-wishers sent gifts of food and he received visits from Ruth and Wootton; there was much media interest in his fate.

Another way he had of 'fighting back' was to smuggle out a statement to the effect that he was responsible for two more murders, of an American pilot and a car mechanic. He tried to get some newspapers interested so he could set up a £25,000 trust fund for his daughter Caroline, the story to break after his expected and imminent death, but, 'For all my resolve, I couldn't just let myself die.' After eighty-four days without food, haunted by the faces of his victims, he ate a bowl of soup on Christmas Day 1979 and confessed that the statement was all lies. He mournfully pondered his fate: 'Who knows what judgement I will receive, when I finally depart this world. I dread to think my torment will continue.'

Roy Fontaine finished his memoirs reflectively:

To any criminal, to anyone who thinks they might have the capacity for murder, to anyone similar to myself, I would urge you not to do it. Think again. In the final analysis my life is an impoverished nightmare. Let me be a lesson to you.

These final words from a serial killer appear discerning and remorseful, written to show that he had never meant any true harm and that, in the end, he resented the nightmare his life had become. Fontaine was careful to portray himself as a likeable rogue, a cunning thief, but not the vicious murderer some would make out. He had, at worst, fallen prey to an uncontrollable anger within him that was fed by his misplaced sense of justice. The murders he committed and his subsequent downfall were brought about by the cruelty and stupidity of others, not by his own actions or malice.

But could a man who carried out such ruthless and cold-blooded killings really have been as innocent as he himself made out? Were the sentiments he expressed so eloquently in his book genuine, or were they simply part of the game of life as played by Archibald Hall/Roy Fontaine, where everything he did and said was simply a means to whatever particular end he had in mind at the time?

Without doubt, Roy Fontaine was a most complex character and through the years – with more than a little help from Fontaine himself – the facts about his life have become almost seamlessly intertwined with fantasy. But who was he really? To find out, we need to re-run the tape and put his story to the test.

PART II:

THE REAL ROY FONTAINE

18

THE MONSTER BUTLER – A SECOND LOOK

The story that Fontaine told in his book appears brutally honest; he could have been whatever he wanted in life, but chose a path that was difficult but glamorous. As for the victims of his thefts, they were legitimate targets who could afford the loss. The brutality of the prison regime hardened him and made him capable of murder, and the greed of David Wright made him first commit the act. Then, once that barrier had been breached, there was no turning back – murder had become a justifiable and necessary resort.

How much of that can be believed?

Fontaine did as he pleased from an early age and successfully manipulated both those who fell for his thin veneer of studied sophistication and those who just happened to be weaker than he was. Like many criminals, Fontaine went to any lengths – including collaborating on writing his life story on at least four occasions – to justify his actions and provide reasons for his failings.

The study of psychopaths has shown that they have an idea they are doing wrong, but have little insight into the effects of their actions on others. Dr Harold Shipman never admitted he enjoyed 'playing God' and acquiring his victims' possessions. Fred West probably hoped that the rest of us might ultimately see him as 'a bit of a lad' who just went a bit too far and at Ian Huntley's trial it was obvious he could not accept he had murdered two young girls to satisfy a sexually-based jealousy tantrum. Indeed, in going to trial, Huntley actually went further than most by disputing the facts and offering a ludicrously feeble explanation for his actions.

An in-depth study raises serious questions about Fontaine's sanity and suggests fantasy was behind much of what he did. His grand plan for self-enrichment was clearly half-baked and does not fully explain what impulse was driving him – was it the need for money, for recognition in elevated social circles or to be regarded as someone very different from his true background, a man with genuine patrician credentials?

The safest standpoint for any study of Fontaine is to ignore much of what he professes to be true and to rely solely on what can be gleaned from historical records and the anecdotal evidence of non-family members. Judging criminal 'success' in terms of today's 'anonymous' drug barons enjoying both wealth and freedom, Fontaine certainly would have been able to plot his spectacularly unsuccessful criminal career by reference to his long list of criminal convictions.

Even so, after the gloss has been stripped from the tale, it still remains remarkable.

If it's true that psychopaths are made and not born, then something affected Fontaine in his early years. His family circumstances might have been the cause of rebellion, but it is also apparent that a significant part of his worldview was inspired by Hollywood – at least some of his criminal behaviour mirroring the celluloid plots of the 1930s, 1940s and 1950s. His adopted sister Violet, who often accompanied him to the cinema in the 1940s, thought that certain films had a peculiar impact on him.

Part of his fascination with the cinema seems to stem from the portrayal of the role of the butler, a common occupation in a bygone age. Perhaps it was the reversal of traditional roles, where a male could be ordered to do something by a more powerful female, that attracted Fontaine to this work. Not only were there persistent hints of sexual familiarity with the lady of the house, but the butler was also often portrayed as the power behind the throne, someone who was indispensable to a wealthy family whose only reason for being rich and powerful was membership of 'the lucky sperm club'. The majority of the cinema-going population naturally empathised with the butler's circumstances, and aware of that fact, Fontaine later dressed up his squalid crimes in an unconvincing 'redistribution of wealth' type disguise.

Of course he never actually trained as a butler, but by the 1950s, the role of the butler was diminishing and employers took what they could get, particularly if the sole applicant for the post could provide flattering, invented references.

In the media reinvention of Fontaine, much has been made of his hard upbringing, his self-taught sophistication and his inherent intelligence, but do such notions really bear scrutiny? Without question he had 'stupid cunning' and was able to exercise characteristic psychopathic control over weaker individuals, some of whom, ultimately, became 'bit players' in his lifelong fantasy of belonging to the fictional rich, carefree aristocracy portrayed in the movies of his adolescent years. But it is his upbringing that provides the first significant clues to the Monster Butler Roy Fontaine would become.

19

YOUNG ROY

Archibald Thomson Hall, Fontaine's father, served with the Royal Corps of Signals during the Great War, and having survived the horror of France and Flanders, took a job with the General Post Office as a sorting clerk and telephonist on demobilisation. He was a man of strong religious conviction, occasionally taking to the pulpit as a lay preacher. Although having east of Scotland origins, he settled in Glasgow where he remained until his death in 1962.

He had married Mary McMillan in January 1924 at Cathedral Street, Glasgow, 'according to the Forms of the United Free Church of Scotland'. His son was born five months later in July 1924, the father being present at the birth. In those days, the stigma of a shotgun wedding cannot be underestimated and it may be that the social pressure to 'do the right thing' came at the cost of parental compatibility.

The boy was an only child until 1931 when Mary – who later liked to be known as Marion – and Archibald senior decided to adopt Violet. Young Archie seems to have been a normal, well-adjusted boy who coped adequately at school and developed into a caring and considerate brother to Violet.

Something, however, seems to have changed the boy's behaviour, something that by the time he was thirteen in 1937 led to the first of his many court appearances. Whatever it was, the boy's father initially blamed the influence of other boys and his solution was to move to a different area of the city, expressly to separate young Archie from friends, although there's also a suggestion of steering clear of gossiping neighbours. Despite comparatively good living conditions, an ostensibly stable family set-up and good schooling, young Archibald – who, like his mother, elected not to use the name he was given and preferred to be known as 'Roy' – was now habitually getting into trouble. He had two separate 'findings of guilt' by 1940 – both when he was thirteen – for malicious mischief and theft and was admonished in both instances. The family had moved house again in 1938 after young 'Roy's' second court appearance, but if the father thought that was the solution to his son's growing criminality, their time at Catterick would leave him with no such hope.

During the Second World War, Archibald Hall senior again answered his country's call and was posted to Catterick Barracks in Yorkshire. His family joined him there but his son's fondness for all things Nazi did not go unnoticed. By that time, young Roy was showing definite signs of going off the rails, and a few months after they had arrived at the base, the Hall family received official visitors.

Suspecting Roy had stolen confidential papers, the Military Police searched the Hall's quarters and found the missing items in his room. They also discovered he had set up a shrine to Hitler, something which at the time was naturally regarded as downright treason, and the Hall family was forced to leave the base in disgrace, returning to Glasgow in 1940.

If Archibald Hall senior had a breaking point, that would surely have been it. It wasn't as if Roy was a child; he was only just short of the age limit for potential basic training for the forces himself, certainly beyond any excuses of naïveté or exemption from harsh punishment. It was also impossible that Marion had not seen the highly offensive memorial to the hated Nazis. Archibald had every right to have lost his temper and cleared the air. In hindsight, he should have, but at the time, something was stopping him. Neither parent seemed willing or able to put an end to their son's wayward behaviour.

Instead, Archibald stoically hid his bitter feelings, returned to his former job and rented a comfortable flat for the family in Cranworth Street near Glasgow University; the Halls never lived in the 'slums' of central Glasgow which compressed nearly three quarters of a million people into a few square miles.

When, at the age of thirty-nine, Marion unexpectedly announced she was pregnant again, Archibald arranged for her confinement at Lindores private clinic in Clairmont Gardens in Glasgow's West End. After his second son, Donald McMillan Thomson Hall was born there on 14 May 1941, Archibald registered the birth as the child's father, but he was not present at the birth as he had been when his first son was born.

In the meantime, rather than showing signs of reform, Roy got into further trouble and in 1941 was given sixty days in jail for two charges of stealing from a house and one charge of uttering a forged cheque. Then in May 1943, he was sentenced to thirty days' imprisonment at Rothesay Sheriff Court for theft and contravening wartime rationing orders. Altering or removing the fashion stigma of the 'utility mark' from clothes and basic goods may not in itself be viewed today as the crime of the century, but it does represent an attempt to outsmart plodding officialdom based on delusional ingenuity. His staunch ally to be, John Wootton, later received six months for fraud at Rothesay Sheriff Court in September 1950, strongly suggesting he went there on Fontaine's recommendation after they met at Wandsworth Prison in 1948. Indeed, Fontaine's vivid descriptions of fictional *Midnight Cowboy* exploits on the Isle of Bute probably persuaded his slow-witted but loyal friend that Rothesay was the place to go to meet wealthy, sexually frustrated older ladies and wide-eyed shopkeepers, who – on account of being separated from the mainland by the Firth of Clyde – were ripe for sophisticated scams by two men such as they.

Both, of course, were rapidly detected and convicted.

In August 1941, when Fontaine was barely seventeen years old, the courts referred him to a psychiatric unit, where he was observed to be apathetic and completely unemotional. He also complained of seeing non-existent people and hearing strange voices, often the symptoms of choice for those eager to opt out of the harsh prison system of the time. He was to receive further psychiatric assessment in 1944 when he was nineteen years old, and this time the examining physicians were more definite. Under the heading 'facts indicating insanity observed by myself' one of them wrote:

> His attitude is abnormal, he postures and grimaces all the time he is being interrogated and his face reflects extreme good humour and pleasure with himself. His diction is most careful and he is evidently anxious to make a good impression, in fact he is almost patronising in his attitude. He is completely without any sense of shame or sorrow for his misdeeds and treats them as if he had not been implicated at all.

She went on to observe, with notable accuracy, 'He gives me the impression that he is acting a part [in] which all the time he is living in a purely imaginary world. He has no moral sense whatever and is a danger to society.'

Between August 1941 and April 1944, the courts referred Fontaine to Hawkhead and Woodilee psychiatric hospitals on three occasions on the grounds of insanity. In those days, it was the rule that if a person who had been committed to an asylum escaped and stayed at large for twenty-eight days, they were effectively discharged. Fontaine successfully made off on each occasion, once whilst 'walking in grounds with his mother', and stayed at large for more than a month each time. It can be reasonably assumed that Marion assisted in these escapes. Whether she was truly unable to recognise the danger her son presented or she simply thought her parental guidance was enough to help him, we will never know.

Whatever the case, it was never long before Fontaine returned to his old ways. In December 1944, he was once more certified insane following court appearances in Dumbarton and Glasgow.

This landed him in Perth Asylum until November 1946, when he was released back into society. It seems clear that his hospital referrals had no corrective effect and their true worth was to record the early warning signs of a dangerous dreamer.

Indeed, Fontaine's failure to mention any of his early offending or psychiatric history casts grave doubts on almost all that is so boldly recorded in *A Perfect Gentleman*. In fact, when his fantastic exploits are looked at in more depth, an entirely different picture emerges.

20

SEXUAL ADVENTURES – PART ONE: MRS PHILIPS, THE POLISH OFFICER AND PICCADILLY CIRCUS

Fontaine went to great lengths to try to convince whoever was prepared to listen that he exuded some sort of magnetic sexual attraction simply by the force of his personality, like his purported idol, Aleister Crowley. Even before he claimed he was seduced by Anne Philips – who was apparently a friend of his mother and almost twice his age – on his sixteenth birthday in 1940, he recalled being in demand from willing young girls.

He described how Anne obviously had designs on him as she arranged a wonderful meal in an exclusive Italian restaurant, the atmosphere heavy with sexual intent, Anne carelessly letting her napkin slip onto the young man's lap, allowing her to fumble meaningfully at his groin. She had also ensured a sophisticated start to the evening by going to the trouble and expense of buying him a dinner jacket. She appears to have been unaffected by wartime deprivation, living well, dressing exquisitely and eating in the best establishments in Glasgow.

His next memorable sexual experience, however, was to be very different. 'Captain Jackobosky', the wartime lodger and Polish freedom fighter was moved into the young Fontaine's double bed and so began Fontaine's initiation into homosexuality, the soldier performing oral sex on him as his family slept nearby. He now 'had the best of both worlds' and he and 'Jackobosky' – who had a privileged background and was the personification of European nobility – spent their time together dining in good restaurants and visiting museums.

After that, he had a constant stream of sexual partners including Vic Oliver, which led to his wartime parties in Ivor Novello's flat where he met Terence Rattigan and others.

Fontaine's early sexual experiences were destined to shape the course of his life, which is, of course, different from giving any credence to his memoirs. The 'older lady' may indeed have existed and very possibly initiated him into the art of lovemaking; his sister Violet later confirmed that a married woman twenty years his senior did 'wine and dine' him despite wartime restrictions and that he spent a lot of time with her, sometimes into the early hours of the morning. Violet also recalled, however, that the lady was popular with many men, which, together with her view that their father was convinced Fontaine was totally infatuated with the woman, puts a different light on things.

What to make of the 'Captain Jackobosky' tale is perhaps more problematical, particularly as many Polish soldiers who had managed to escape from the Soviets and the Nazis actually did end up billeting in the very area of Glasgow's West End that Fontaine's parents' spacious flat was in.

His early sexual tutors, it seems, had to be 'sophisticated', and apart from preying on young boys, the handsome Pole was also prepared to 'wine and dine' the teenage Fontaine before giving him tuition in, amongst other things, 'culture'. Why Marion would suggest that a solution for the foreign soldier's nocturnal discomfort was for him to share her young son's bed is difficult to fathom, the obvious answer being for the pair to swap bedrooms. It might even be that Fontaine got some of the image of 'Jackobosky' from a film, something he was unquestionably prone to doing.

Sir Terence Rattigan, who apparently continually pestered Fontaine for sex, was probably the most successful playwright of his generation, two of his plays running for more than 1000 performances in the West End. The author of *The Winslow Boy* and *French Without Tears* – the title of which was mimicked by

Aleister Crowley in *Magick Without Tears* – came from military stock, but after the turmoil of his education at Harrow and Trinity College, Oxford, he emerged to become a dramatist. In the Oxford of his day, it was fashionable for young male under-graduates to affect foppish mannerisms and camp behaviour. In Rattigan's case, the fashionable behaviour of the time helped mask the fact that he was actively homosexual, but of course, a public admission of such at that time would have damaged his career.

As with all the men Fontaine cites as gay lovers in the 1950s and 1960s, not only were their sexual proclivities either well known and tacitly accepted or guessed at, but also none of them, of course, were alive when he co-wrote his biography. Rattigan died in 1977, Sir Beverley Baxter died in 1964 and Lord Mountbatten, First Earl Mountbatten of Burma and former Governor General of India, was murdered by the IRA aged seventy-nine in 1979. Ivor Novello, the composer of the song *Keep The Home Fires Burning*, died in 1951. He was as openly gay as was then possible and lived with his lover for many years.

All of these men were rich and successful in their own right, whether by birth, by dint of talent or both. Fontaine seems to have craved their lifestyles and social standing, and it would appear unlikely that even if he had been in their company, he would have been regarded as the 'well bred young gentleman' he sought to be. Moreover, it's hard to imagine someone like Fontaine not exploiting the social vulnerability of the men he names by stealing from them in anticipation of their silence should he be suspected.

His alleged closeness with Rattigan is highly dubious but it may be that Fontaine's propensity to fantasise and exaggerate masks the truth and suggests that he may have been earning money for sexual favours at that time of his life.

As for the stated meeting with Vic Oliver in Glasgow's Central Hotel in 1942, the surrounding circumstances appear improb-able; the young lone diner is invited to join the well-known celebrity for dinner, which then leads to a lasting friendship. Vic Oliver was a Jewish entertainer who had fled his native Austria to pursue a career in Britain and America. He had the 'distinction' of being on the 'liquidation list' the Nazis prepared before the proposed invasion of Britain.

Fontaine wrote:

A few years later my male lover, Vic Oliver became the son-in-law of the great Winston Churchill. What the great man would have thought of his son-in-law had he known of his propensity for loitering around gents' toilets, I dread to think.

Fontaine's timing is out if he thought his 'lover' married Sarah Churchill 'a few years later' as he actually married her in 1936 (when Fontaine was only twelve), and they were divorced by 1945.

And what Churchill thought of his son-in-law is, in fact, documented. At dinner one evening, Churchill was asked whom he particularly admired and, surprisingly, he answered, 'Mussolini.' When asked why he made that improbable choice – and within earshot of Oliver – he said, 'Because he had the good sense to shoot his son-in-law!'

It is impossible to ascertain how many of Fontaine's recollections of early sexual exploits are true. If anything can be judged from his proven exaggerations elsewhere, it is fair to say that few of his boasted sexual adventures with the rich and famous of wartime Glasgow and London can be believed. However, whatever truth exists in these stories, it is clear that from a young age Fontaine was learning to use his sexuality to try to manipulate others.

21

THE MOWBRAY HOUSE JOB – THE TRUTH

Fontaine's Version:

He was the mastermind and main actor; Wootton played the other, lesser part in the scheme, distracting the shop owner on the phone and driving the getaway car; Fontaine planted phone directories in the deed box after taking the jewels. It was the biggest jewel raid in Scotland at the time to the tune of £100,000 and they became folk heroes; even the Chief Constable met their train when it arrived in Edinburgh; at court Fontaine pleaded guilty to let his mother go free and allow Wootton to plead to a lesser charge.

Fontaine claimed he first met Esta Henry at an auction in Glasgow at a time when he was running a small second-hand shop and she was the owner of an internationally renowned jewellery and antiques business at Mowbray House in Edinburgh's Royal Mile. Despite their different business interests, she was impressed from the start by his charm, wit and impressive knowledge of silver, precious stones and antiques in general.

Or so he claimed.

One of the confidence tricks that the tabloids later so admired was Fontaine's claim that he had attended the Holyroodhouse Garden Party in place of his employer Mr Warren-Connell in 1953, just a short distance from Mrs Henry's shop. Particularly in those days, the Garden Party invitation was social prestige of the highest order and was issued only to a select group. Fontaine mingled with society's top rank and drank expensive bubbly before going to visit Esta – whom he refers to as 'Esther' – at her business close by. There, he presented her with a dozen red roses and recorded that she was 'most impressed' not only by his visit but by the fact that he had been at the exclusive event nearby.

In reality, it has to be wondered why 'Esther' failed to recognise him as the second-hand shop owner from Glasgow, or indeed what she, as the owner of such a prestigious outlet, was doing at a Glasgow auction in the company of dealers in stolen goods. The timing of the situation – while the Warren-Connells were conveniently on holiday – is also suspect. For instance, why did Mr Warren-Connell's invitation arrive so close to the date of the function itself? It is also interesting that not only was the invitation apparently extended solely to Mr Warren-Connell, but also that the family was completely unaware of the likelihood of their attendance that year.

Fontaine's 'memory' of attending the Garden Party seems to have little chance of being true. His version of the theft from Mowbray House, however, *can* be shown to be complete fabrication. It is true that he was involved. And when he, Wootton and a mysterious third man with the unlikely name of 'Ross-Wham' raided Mowbray House on 11 March 1953, it was obvious they at least had a working knowledge of Mrs Henry's shop practices, particularly as to where she kept her more expensive pieces. Journalistic legend had it that she had recently purchased some of the deposed King Farouk of Egypt's treasure trove, which included part of the original Hungarian Crown Jewels.

That his appearance at the High Court at Edinburgh in July 1953 is a matter of public record seems to have had no bearing on Fontaine's later claims about the case, as rather than being the mastermind and thief, it appears his role was peripheral.

Together with Wootton and George Ross-Wham, he was indicted for trial on 30 July 1953, the charge reading as follows:

On 11 March 1953 in the shop occupied by Esta Louis or Henry at 51 High Street Edinburgh [they did] steal £325 of money, 600 American Dollars, 24 brooches, 9 rings, 10 necklaces, a medallion, 6 pendants, 16 pairs of ear-rings, a gold frame, 18 vinaigrettes, a walking stick head, a quantity of bracelets, a Frobisher box in case, a gold heart, a fleur-de-lis, a cigarette case, 7 watches, a gold guard, a quantity of opals and crystal drops, a prong hairpin, a quantity of tissue paper, 2 pieces of cloth, 2 keys on a chain, a cigar box, 2 couchettes, 7 jewel boxes, a jewel case, a ring box, 2 jewel holdalls, 6 elastic bands, 2 price tags, a collection of 8 paste brooches and pendants, a collection of 5 heart shaped pendants, a seed pearl guard, a pair of pear shaped pearls, a guard chain, 2 ropes of pearls, 10 Deposit Receipts, a quantity of private letters, business cards and private papers and a brooch of three aquamarines.

After all three accused had appeared at the first diet of the case on 20 July, 'Ross-Wham' failed to appear at the trial ten days later. Curiously, the prosecution moved for a warrant for his apprehension but not for forfeiture of the bail money of £250, which had been lodged to ensure his attendance at all diets of the case. The explanation seems to have been that the third accused was in custody in England at the time, but it turns out he never actually appeared again to face the charge, so his role in the proceedings is intriguing.

Counsel for Wootton, who also acted for Fontaine (a quirk of the times), intimated that Wootton would plead guilty to the theft of items totalling £1500 and Fontaine would plead to receiving stolen goods to the value of £800, all of which had been recovered. The pleas having been accepted, the court was told that property to the value of £5000 had been stolen that day, consisting of money and jewellery.

The prosecutor said that it was obvious the three accused must have been going in and out the shop for some time as they had a good knowledge of the lay-out. Mrs Henry had been in the shop on her own that day and two of the accused, posing as Americans, had entered and shown interest in a silver Georgian tea set. In the course of negotiations, the telephone rang and the caller asked to speak to one of the men in the shop. A little later it rang again and this time the caller enquired about a tea set and Mrs Henry noticed one of the men examining candlesticks at the front of the shop. The other man at the back of the shop must have been the one who emptied the contents of the deed box into the case he was carrying and replaced them with items from a nearby shelf.

After the two men left, Mrs Henry noticed the items from the shelf were missing and she originally reported *their* disappearance to the police. It turned out they had not been stolen but had been put in the deed box to replace the items actually taken. There was no mention of telephone directories.

The stolen items had been sold by Fontaine and Wootton in London, Paignton and Canterbury, where they were arrested on 30 April 1953. Counsel told the court that Fontaine was an antiques dealer who had no part in the incidents in the shop and that Wootton had been trying to lead an honest life after his release from prison, but his criminal past had caught up with him and 'embarrassed' him.

Lord Keith sentenced Wootton to four years' and Fontaine to three years' imprisonment.

Had the matter gone to trial, witnesses from Edinburgh, Langholm in Dumfriesshire, Chelsea, Brighton, Paignton, Canterbury, Torquay and Ramsgate would have been called by the prosecution and it's worth noting that one of the Ramsgate witnesses was Fontaine's mother.

The stories Fontaine spun – both in his own two memoirs and in interviews he offered to other writers – always vary in detail and there are various accounts of the theft from Mowbray House, but it has to be assumed that what was said in court about how the raid was carried out is likely to be closer to the truth than his own egocentric accounts.

Whilst his mother was never an accused, as he alleged, it

might have been that the police hinted at her being charged with something to force his and Wootton's hand, but he certainly did not 'take the rap' as he fondly and nobly recalls.

Indeed, as can be seen, Fontaine squirmed out on a lesser charge and instructed counsel that he was an unfortunate antiques dealer who had 'nothing to do with' events in the shop. The 'telephone directories for jewels' tale makes the scheme sound more sophisticated than it really was and puts a gloss on what was an opportunistic sneak theft, although the knowledge of the whereabouts of the deed box and the diversionary phone calls show some basic planning.

If he had known or indeed cultivated Mrs Henry before the theft and if he and Wootton had been in the shop memorising the layout, she would surely have recognised him, making his apprehension inevitable. The narration in court also makes it clear that Fontaine was the annoying caller from the public call box, rather than the daring jewel thief the unwitting shopkeeper smiled at as he left and tipped his hat.

Despite Fontaine's oft-proclaimed and 'principled' standpoint of refusing to 'grass' on fellow conspirators, he seems to have had no compunction in rapidly informing the investigating officers that Ross-Wham or 'Ricky' as he knew him, was the third man and that he had received forty-five pieces of jewellery as his share. Wootton likewise told police that Ross-Wham had been involved, and he confirmed that he was the one who had actually stolen the jewellery. Wootton also said he had received a mere £208 as his share of the loot and Ross-Wham told police he had only received a miserable £140 despite being the actual thief.

Ross-Wham also said he had met Fontaine through Wootton and that they had all discussed the scheme, but when he had actually visited the shop on his own, he was against going ahead with it.

By chance he met Wootton again and was eventually persuaded to take part in the raid, travelling from London on 10 March 1953 and staying at the Melville Castle Hotel in

Lasswade, Midlothian, the night before the theft. He was the one who had taken the items from the shelf to place in the deed box 'to make up the weight', which tallies with the police enquiry.

One revealing detail the elusive Ross-Wham mentioned, though, was the fact that Fontaine sat in the rear of the getaway car and it was he who 'divided' the loot up. If indeed they did get away with anything like the amount Fontaine later boasted about, which is very unlikely, one of the three thieves appears to have done considerably better than the other two – namely the one who apportioned the loot!

22

THE TROUBLE WITH JUSTICE . . .
THE MONTAGUE ARMS AND
THE 'HENLEY' BREAK-INS

Fontaine's Version:

He met a drunken barmaid who told him about the set up in the pub; he carried out the job with a safe blower and they were careful to ensure there would be no forensic evidence. In the 'Henley' break-in, he again met a girl who spoke about her employer's valuables; he broke in twice, having failed to find main cache the first time.

Fontaine was released from the three-year sentence from Edinburgh High Court in late 1955 but, in typical fashion, was quickly back in trouble. In truth, he was capable only of short periods of liberty, during which no thought was given to anything other than petty thievery whilst concurrently plotting implausible scams. He was out only a few months when he earned himself the first of the particularly heavy sentences that were to categorise and shape his life to the end.

He had made an immediate return to thieving on his release from prison. His first hit was a hotel in Slough, Buckinghamshire. Whilst probably unaware of Sir John Betjeman's 1937 exhortation to blow up the town and its 'bogus-Tudor bars', Fontaine and a colleague instead blew up the safe at the Montague Arms Hotel.

The tale recounted by Fontaine forty years after the event

was colourful and entertaining, with its befriended watchdog and his own forensic awareness; it would certainly have been of interest to the prosecution at his trial, where he stoutly proclaimed his innocence.

The proceedings were reported by the *Guardian* on 4 January 1956. It noted that Fontaine was, again, an 'antiques dealer' and that he was convicted of blowing the safe and stealing £450, despite pleading not guilty. The safe-blower Carr, however, had tendered a plea of guilty to the charge and somehow had been prevailed upon by Fontaine to give evidence on his behalf!

The prosecution evidence was that police had found two pairs of trousers in Fontaine's Knightsbridge flat that linked him to the Montague Arms safe blowing. After tests, one of them was found to have traces of gelignite on them and the other traces of safe ballast, obviously suspicious facts that most juries would require answers to.

However, when Carr gave evidence he followed the only line Fontaine wanted him to, which was to try to convince the jury that he, Carr, had acted alone in committing the crime. How Fontaine pressured his co-accused into taking all the blame, with the risk of receiving a stiffer sentence, can only be guessed at.

Then, desperately trying to pretend that the damning clothing did not belong to him, Fontaine came up with a gambit many years ahead of – and not nearly as successful as – that employed by O.J. Simpson's legal team, when he sought and was granted permission to leave the dock in order to try on both pairs of trousers, presumably to try to show that they were ill-fitting and so did not belong to him.

Accordingly, he left the dock and tried the first pair on, and on his return the newspaper reported that he was displaying 'an expanse of leg'. No doubt hamming it up, Fontaine then returned wearing the second pair, which he appeared to be holding up at the waist in order to suggest they were too big for him.

Probably not for the first time in his thirty-one years, he must have experienced a warm glow thinking that he had hoodwinked a jury of his peers, only to be quickly brought crashing back down to earth. Whether they disliked his arrogant playacting or simply had a collective nose for the antics of an incorrigible conman, they decided to call his bluff. Obviously unconvinced that his demonstration was credible, they asked to examine the trousers he was actually wearing in court so that a proper comparison could be made with the two pairs recovered from his flat. So, no doubt with a sinking feeling, Fontaine was obliged to remove his trousers again and await his fate.

It didn't take the jury long to conclude that all three pairs were the same size and he was duly convicted and given ten years' 'preventive detention', Carr receiving seven years' imprisonment.

The trial demonstrated, yet again, Fontaine's ability to manipulate co-accused into either taking more than their share of the blame, or of actively twisting the facts to try to assist him in saving his own skin. The true story also shows that rather than being careful to avoid leaving 'police forensics', he was trapped by carelessly leaving the contaminated clothing at his flat.

The other offence of breaking and entering Fontaine remembered at that time took place at Henley and involved yet another beautiful young woman eager to impart intimate details to him whilst under the influence of drink. This time, it was the *au pair* to the rich family who were about to go on holiday. He claimed he broke in and stole an ornate Renaissance Spanish galleon encrusted in rubies and diamonds, and then – a part of the story that *can* be verified – with breathtaking impertinence and stupidity, took the object to Esta Henry's son's shop in Edinburgh where he attempted to sell it to him.

According to Fontaine, Louis, Esta's son, offered him £2000 for it but this was refused as being well below the true value, so he left and quickly hid the object. Later that same day, the Edinburgh police – Fontaine claims that it was again Mr Merrilees, the Chief Constable himself – came to his hotel room and searched it but found nothing.

Undeterred, Fontaine simply returned to Henley and broke into the house a second time, this time finding the jewel box he had been looking for during the first break-in, which he then placed in a safety deposit box in Harrods.

The *Guardian*, which might be more reliable than *A Perfect Gentleman*, reported that the break-in had in fact been at Harlow in Essex, but it too mentioned the offer of a stolen *objet d'art* to Louis Henry who later recounted what had actually occurred.

Sure enough, Fontaine and another man had entered his shop in Edinburgh's Hanover Street offering to sell a Renaissance jewel-encrusted pendant in the shape of George and the Dragon. He obviously concluded that it would have been impossible for Fontaine to have legitimate possession of such an item, so he contacted the police who then interviewed Fontaine and his accomplice. At that stage, however, there was insufficient evidence to charge them with theft, but it was a different matter when the authorities were able to piece events together at a later date, leading to his arrest soon after.

Perhaps seeking sympathy of some kind, he later bemoaned English justice, claiming that he received thirty-five years in January 1956 at Aylesbury Quarter Sessions, comprising three sentences of ten years for housebreakings and one of five years for possessing a firearm.

As we have seen, though, his previous convictions record that he was sentenced to ten years apiece for two housebreakings and five years for the firearms offence, the sentences to run *concurrently*, meaning a cumulo ten-year sentence and not the thirty-five he implied nor the fifteen he claimed.

His fulminations against English justice might be better understood if it could be shown that he had actually been innocent of the charges, or even that he intended turning over a new leaf on his release from his previous sentence. It should also have occurred to him, but obviously did not, that trying to sell a unique stolen artefact to someone whose mother you have stolen from in the past showed particular stupidity. In Fontaine's case, however, none of those were considerations.

23

SEXUAL ADVENTURES – PART TWO: THE DAYS OF GENUINE POLITICAL SCANDAL

As we have seen, Fontaine's compulsion to exaggerate what he regarded as his achievements extended to his self-proclaimed attraction to both sexes. His stories of his sexual activities in the 1950s, however, continued as per those from his youth – mainly highly implausible and full of uncanny coincidences when compared with outside sources.

He recounted that in 1952, when working as a butler to a rich family in Dunblane, his employer walked in on him servicing their young Swedish *au pair* from behind – naturally called Agnetha – and he was summarily dismissed, but not before he rightfully demanded proper compensation, which he then used to treat the enthusiastic Scandinavian to a fortnight of pleasure in the sun. Wootton, however, later confirmed that Fontaine had never been a butler in Dunblane, that he had a kitchen job at a girls' school there and that he, Wootton, was accused by Marion of having an affair with a German girl who worked there as well.

There was constant prison sex too – not just with prisoners and not just with male partners. When he had the good fortune to be transferred to an all-female prison, he and a female prisoner were able to synchronise visits to the bin area where they would have sex against the large rubbish containers before going their separate ways back to the segregated sections of the prison.

When at liberty, his talent for meeting famous public figures was remarkable. As with Vic Oliver and others, he happened to meet the broadcaster and entertainer Gilbert Harding – probably best known for being the irascible presenter of the 1950s show *What's My Line?* – when he was frequenting the Montague Arms in Slough with a view to emptying the safe.

However, Harding's homosexuality was well known and referred to as 'confirmed bachelorhood' in those days, and while Fontaine mentions Harding by name, he mysteriously fails to name his partner. It's likely he actually never met either of them but heard rumours that they stayed locally.

Another of Fontaine's more outrageous stories is that, while on a foreign holiday, he met and serviced a married lady. Then, when her husband found out, he was jealous rather than outraged, and Fontaine calmed the situation with an impromptu threesome.

And then there was Lord Boothby.

Fontaine claimed that, having placed the jewels stolen from the house in Harlow in a Harrods safety deposit box – where else? – he dropped into the nearby Green Man Bar where he met Boothby who invited him back to his flat and then into his bed. Afterwards, as they chatted, Fontaine noticed pictures of Churchill, the Kray twins and Dorothy Macmillan – wife of the former prime minister Harold Macmillan – bedecked round the room. When Fontaine mentioned his need for a foreign holiday, Boothby immediately recommended a beautiful flat in Antibes owned by Somerset Maugham's gay lover 'Peter Seals'. Soon thereafter, Fontaine flew out and indulged in an orgy of sunshine, gambling, drink and sex with the male guests and the houseboys who looked after them.

Robert (later Lord) Boothby was Conservative MP for East Aberdeenshire for many years until 1958 and at one stage, was Churchill's private secretary. His cousin, Ludovic Kennedy, who died in October 2009, claimed that Boothby fathered children with at least two married women he was having affairs with, and it was generally known – in the days when 'the establishment looked after its own and the press looked the other way' – that he had a long-standing affair with Dorothy Macmillan.

Another open secret was that Boothby was bisexual and that one of his lovers was Ronnie Kray, one half of the notorious gangster duo from the 1960s.

His relationship with Kray had serious political implications when the left-leaning *Sunday Mirror* published a story about it in July 1964. However, when Boothby threatened to sue, the paper's editor suddenly lost his nerve and settled out of court. Boothby received the not inconsiderable sum, for those days, of £40,000 and a confidentiality clause further suppressed the truth that Boothby and Kray *had* been lovers as well as joint attendees at 'rent boy' parties.

The opposition Labour Party were unable to make any political capital out of the story at the time, mainly, it was thought, due to the outrageous behaviour of the eccentric Labour MP Tom Driberg, later Baron Bradwell, which stopped the Labour leader Harold Wilson from exploiting the situation for fear of inciting a retributive attack.

Wilson's lack of action is easily understandable, as Driberg's antics probably put Boothby's in the shade – he was reputed to have been anointed by the 'Great Beast' Aleister Crowley as his successor in the black arts, and was forced to take cover in the then customary 'highly public wedding' after a rapid succession of homosexual affairs. He was a close friend of the spy Guy Burgess and was rumoured to have been a Soviet spy himself, having been compromised by engaging in homosexual behaviour with a KGB operative.

Fontaine's 'encounter' with Boothby might have had more credibility had he not immediately referred to the bedside photographs, making the story read as a thinly veiled rehash of well-churned rumours. Indeed, the surprise is that Fontaine failed to mention Driberg in his memoirs. Legend has it that the police in Westminster often had to search for and retrieve him from nearby gents' toilets whenever an important Commons vote was imminent. Again, Churchill's wry comments are worth relating; of Driberg he is said to have observed, 'He gives sodomy a bad name.'

Fontaine's fabulous holiday on the Cote d'Azur, concocted solely on the strength of a one-off encounter with a new friend, is far-fetched, particularly as Maugham allowed only literary figures – or fellow former secret agents – to holiday at Villa Mauresque where he died in December 1965; his partner who inherited the contents of the villa was actually called Alan Searle.

Yet again, Fontaine exhibited his innate ability to dream up the most unlikely sexual scenarios. His desire to be recognised as someone who was attractive and sophisticated enough to catch the attention of the rich and powerful grows ever more blatant as his life story progresses. With each 'memory' he adds another layer to his crafted persona until he thinks he has successfully established himself in his readers' minds as the handsome and daring thief he believed, or at least wanted others to believe, he was.

24

SUBLIME SCAMS

Fontaine's Version:

The sheik scam: Procured Arab wear from costumier; hired Rolls-Royce and driver; made phone calls to 'sheik' from outside; moved from hotel to hotel then the sting took place at the Dorchester.

Other scams: Switched copied rings; used a fake 'fiancée' ruse; carried out a raid at 'Gerrards'.

Spending so much of his time in prison, Fontaine seems to have whiled away the long days either by having sex with other prisoners or by telling tales of his exploits hoodwinking the owners of expensive gems. As is often said in court, sometimes the best witnesses are those who genuinely believe what they say, which, of course, is entirely different from whatever the truth might be.

For Fontaine, telling lies came naturally. Prison brought the opportunity not only to cultivate his exaggerated tales but also to spin them to an audience from which he needed neither sanction nor credulity. By the time he received the 'natural life' sentence at the Old Bailey in 1978, he had built up a reputation – within the prison system at least – as the daring butler who fleeced the wealthy and who was responsible for brilliant thefts and robberies.

The reputation was initially self-created, but, no doubt to his delight, was avidly taken up and embroidered in some areas of the press. Thus, by the time his biography was published in 1999, the most fantastic and incredible heists and feats of derring-do in the manly pursuit of jewels were listed without irony or fear of derision. Encouraging Fontaine to 'embellish' on his largely unsuccessful criminal career was pretty unsavoury, but neither he nor those seeking sensational stories were bound by such constraints. By that time, of course, he was beyond both ridicule and redemption.

Of all the schemes, real or imagined, that he and others attributed to his criminal genius, the 'sheik impersonation' is the one that is the most enthusiastically recounted with a fervour bordering on veneration. Undoubtedly, Fontaine was more than capable of inventing zany ways of relieving the gullible of their possessions, but the sheik scam from the 1950s has to be seen as something dreamed up in the knowledge that no-one would be likely to take it seriously, at first anyway. Successfully impersonating a real sheik, he convinced six jewellers to hand their gems into a steam filled room just before he slipped out of his robes and made off in his business suit with £300,000 worth of goods. To perfect matters even further, he was never questioned or charged with the spectacular crime.

Clearly, the police dismally failed in their duty to investigate it, neither checking with costumiers nor hirers of prestige cars; they even forgot to take fingerprints. How Fontaine managed to 'bombard' his own suite with outside calls is unexplained, as is how he was able to flee with £300,000 worth of gems wearing a presumably saturated lounge suit without drawing attention to himself. Succeeding in congregating six dim-witted jewellers with no idea of the layout of the suite also shows astonishing good fortune in the execution of the plan.

A second version of the tale involved him carrying out the whole plan in just one day and in this one, the duped salesmen were informed at reception that he was bathing, so upon visiting his room, all they ever saw was a falsely tanned arm which extended from the steam of the room to whisk away the valuable gems for ever.

Curiously, in Fontaine's 1981 biography, *The Prison Cell Confessions of Archibald Thompson Hall*, there is no mention of the 'sheik' business, which, if it were true, would surely enliven any life story, so its omission casts all the more doubt on its veracity.

A variation on the theme, he later claimed, was when he managed to entice a luckless jewel salesman into his suite at an Edinburgh hotel in 1966 in order to view some rings as a surprise birthday present for his sleeping wife. The shop's representative was picked up in a hired Rolls-Royce and whisked off to the hotel where, on his arrival, Fontaine poured him a large whisky before disappearing into the suite's 'bedroom' to show his wife the rings. The plot ends with a disorientated salesman asking at reception for persons long gone from the hotel.

That variation does have certain elements that match the charges he faced at Edinburgh High Court in 1966 when he was indicted for not paying for his lodgings at a hotel, not paying for the hire of a chauffeur-driven car and, somewhat mundanely, snatching a tray of rings from a jeweller's shop in Paisley. There was no mention of any charge regarding a well-executed sting operation involving fabulous gems, only a litany of tawdry small-time offences.

He was fond of making out that he had the ability to study rings and jewels with an eye expert enough to have exact copies made up later, sometimes at a cost to himself of hundreds of pounds. These were then swapped over on a subsequent visit to the shop when different assistants were working. Similarly, he said he employed the same tactic when working for rich families, the copies being so exact, the over-indulged owners failed to spot the switch. In reality, it is highly unlikely that his appraisal skills could outwit the owner of some treasured possession, let alone a trained jeweller.

The other trick was to take a 'fiancée' along to the shop and persuade the sales staff of the need to view the ring in daylight. Once outside, Fontaine would drop his lighter, at which point the salesperson, anxious to make the sale, would quickly bend over to retrieve it. In the meantime, Fontaine and his athletic sidekick would make off to a waiting car driven by Wootton.

Where he was able to recruit such nimble actors who steadfastly stuck to a collective vow of silence down the years was never revealed. Nor was just how pursuing sales staff either fell for the schoolboyish ploy or failed to note the registration number of the getaway car.

An accomplice was also required for another scheme, which involved Fontaine confidentially revealing an aristocratic title to the receptionist when checking into a hotel and requesting anonymity during his stay. His hope, however, seems to be short-lived when another guest recognises him, loudly announces his title when greeting him, and demands they celebrate their chance meeting with a round of drinks. The purpose of it all was apparently to 'soften up' the staff to readily accepting a dud cheque or two from the shy aristocrat. On the contrary, it might be thought that such a laboured charade would have the opposite effect of alerting staff and jeopardising a successful outcome.

Another of Fontaine's extravagant claims involved a daring heist at one of London's most illustrious jewellers. According to Fontaine, the meticulous and daring raid on the jeweller's shop in London's Regent Street involved switching the alarms on and off at precisely agreed times. Once again, no mention was made of police interest in what would have been a substantial haul involving intensive planning and specialised knowledge, particularly for someone on the run at the time. As an inside job, there should have been no difficulty in tracing at least one member of the gang, so the lack of investigation has to be a mystery.

Another mystery is that, having he been involved in the spectacular raid, he recalls the name of the shop to be 'Gerrards' rather than 'Garrard'.

It is certainly obvious that Fontaine had a vivid imagination that he put to good use in seeking to establish himself as an acknowledged master jewel thief. The fact that there is little or no evidence to support his stories – on the contrary most of the court records portray him as a petty thief at best – mattered little to Fontaine. The only true picture of the man that we can gain from his own accounts of these implausible scams is one of a manipulative individual willing to go to any lengths to secure admiration and respect.

25

A PROLIFIC PAROLE

After his release in March 1963 from his sentence for the Montague Arms and Henley break-ins, Fontaine was at liberty for a mere ten months. His next sentence would be for ten years and again it involved 'preventive detention'. In England, the term described a sentence imposed on 'habitual criminals' who had accrued at least three convictions since the age of sixteen and, when first implemented, usually entailed penal servitude and a period of hard labour. Fontaine still had eight months of parole to serve from his previous sentence, imposed at Aylesbury in 1956, when he received the next ten years for theft at the Old Bailey in January 1964.

His first task on his release was to act as best man at his mother's wedding to John Wootton at Stafford Registry Office in March 1963. It has to be wondered whether the happy couple waited on his release out of respect, fear or expediency as both the best man and the groom had just been liberated from custodial sentences. The new Mrs Wootton had always been less than discouraging towards her son's selfish behaviour and the new stepfather had gone to any lengths to assist him in his criminal enterprises – and there were some spectacular examples to come – so it was not to be anticipated that either the bride or the groom might be the conduit to an improvement in Fontaine's conduct.

Indeed, Wootton, who can safely be seen as one of life's followers, had also tried the 'butler routine' and with the same inevitable outcome, his copycat frauds in 1950s Rothesay failing to make him realise that Fontaine's criminal tuition was better ignored. Wootton had taken a butler's post at Haddon Hall in Derbyshire where he stole and sold some of his employer's antique furniture, which was rapidly traced back to its rightful owner. Realising he was about to be apprehended, Wootton took off with Marion to Saltcoats in Ayrshire, for reasons best known to themselves, where he was arrested. Donald too had got into bother for pestering a girl in a cinema there – another factor Fontaine later used to 'justify' his murder in 1978 – but he was subjected only to a police warning; Wootton was sentenced to six years at Derby Crown Court.

Wedding receptions are often eclectic gatherings of persons who otherwise might prefer to be elsewhere, but the Wootton nuptials guest list and reception reads like a screenplay for an Ealing Comedy. Fontaine, of course, confronted the 'guest' he had served time with in Winchester Prison whom he suspected had 'dipped' the blushing bride's purse for a few hundred pounds on the day of the ceremony. He searched him, found nothing and told him to 'fuck off' as he had 'stolen from his own'.

Compared to English justice, Fontaine's version had a much lower standard of proof, and his rule about not harming 'your own' obviously did not personally apply to him. As we have seen before, Fontaine had no problem tipping the scales in his favour at others' expense, and these exceptions certainly extended to those he deemed worthy. After all, the wedding money had come from his deceased father's estate, Marion having *requested* and received £200 from her sons to 'make up for' her omission from Archibald's will.

After a few weeks staying with the newly married couple, Fontaine was up to his old tricks. He inveigled his way into a domestic post with a disabled American who lived in Hastings, Sussex, and whilst there he met and charmed the resident cook, Phylis Nye, into jointly applying for residential posts elsewhere. Never short of confidence, he advertised in *The Times* and incredibly, offers started coming in.

The pair eventually settled for posts with the retired diplomat Nigel Law and his family in Chalfont St Peter, Buckinghamshire. Before long, Fontaine noticed that his employer had omitted the soup spoons from the silver inventory and these were quickly turned into hard cash.

The next posts were with Sir George and Lady Aylwen, he being the former Lord Mayor of London. Fontaine – yet again – claimed to have been in the right place at the right time when his prospective employer telephoned the Laws to check on the references submitted and, once more, he was able to effect a convincing impromptu impersonation of his employer in order to secure the post.

His stay with the Aylwens was short, less than five weeks. He later wrote about how much Lady Aylwen liked him and about having masochistic sex with her Ladyship, stealing jewellery and, of course, copying the safe key.

In reality, the great lover and jewel thief was sacked after that time and all the Aylwens could report stolen was a leather purse worth £15. Lady Aylwen sensed something sinister about him – particularly when her husband was in hospital for a few days – to the extent that just after she dismissed him she part-wrote a play about an evil butler, but it was never produced.

One of Fontaine's major boasts, of course, was that he once worked for Sir Charles Clore, the rich financier, which was true. His employment lasted a mere five days from 10 to 15 November 1963, during which time Clore, too, had his doubts. His new butler was too glib and, despite what appeared to be excellent references, seemed fairly useless at his job.

Another of Clore's employees, Mr Kay, who was tasked with supervising the new butler, noticed Fontaine pouring water for a guest, then, instead of replacing the jug on the serving table as a proper butler would have done, he simply dumped it down on the highly polished dinner table surface. It was a rudimentary gaffe even for an untrained member of staff, let alone a highly recommended butler. Kay was in a difficult situation with both the guest and his employer, so he apologised to Sir Charles for the new man's solecism.

Sir Charles then reputedly observed, 'He's no more a butler than I am!'

Fontaine's true past was revealed when Clore called in Scotland Yard, the Laws and other employers discovered their losses and he was soon back in court for the ten-year sentence imposed in 1964.

Naturally, Fontaine had an alternative version of events.

His departure from the Clore household after only five days was *not* down to incompetence but to insurance investigators discovering his true identity. If he was, as he claimed, 'only a whisker away from his biggest robbery' when he was sacked, then Sir Charles Clore must have been naïve in the extreme, something he was rarely accused of.

Fontaine obviously saw buttling as an opportunity to line his pockets, although being associated with the rich and famous probably appealed to him as well. His thin veneer of politeness and manners sometimes allowed him to scrape by, but in truth he was unlikely to survive the mildest of domestic tests.

26

ESCAPE TO LARCENY

The imposition of ten years' preventive detention in January 1964 should have protected society – and even 'high society' – from Fontaine's predations for a while, but it wasn't to be. He was sent to Blundeston Prison near Lowestoft in Suffolk, which was regarded as virtually escape-proof. One of the few skills Fontaine was actually very good at was escaping and not only did he and two others, Donald Whitaker and George Thomas Patrick O'Neill, break out against all odds, but he actually *was* on the run in Scotland and England from September 1965 until May 1966. The three escapees made it from Suffolk to Scotland by stealing vehicles and, of course, getting help from Wootton and others. Once again, Fontaine mentions a crime the police showed no apparent interest in, namely the raid on a bookie's house which involved them impersonating the CID. When the lady of the house asked to see their search warrant, Fontaine was forced to concede that none existed, then apologised for 'robbing' them; the victims were apparently unable to take action over their ordeal as the bookie was actually 'fencing' stolen goods. And once again, the haul was worthwhile, the raid earning them a few thousand pounds each.

Naturally, he claims the other two escapees were recaptured well before him, but following his arrest, he was again indicted at Edinburgh High Court where the indictment noted that O'Neill and Whitaker's addresses were 'to the Prosecutor unknown', suggesting *they* were the ones who were still at large. The date was 13 May 1966 and he was described as a 'general dealer aged forty-one of no fixed abode'. The indictment itself makes interesting reading and illustrates just how low Britain's self-proclaimed 'top jewel thief' was prepared to stoop; that said, it's also remarkable what he and the others actually did when officially on the run.

The first charge related to the three escapees stealing a car from a Mr Gregory at his quaintly named Toad Hall residence in Halesworth, Suffolk, and was triable in Scotland under the Larceny Act of 1916 which permitted jurisdiction to be established by proving possession in one part of the United Kingdom of items allegedly stolen in another.

The second related to the reset – the receiving of stolen items – of a driving licence and three cheque books belonging to a Mr Hindley from Lancashire. Charge three involved using these to fraudulently hire a car and procure lodging at the expensive Central Hotel in Glasgow, which, of course, would be one of the last places the authorities would expect to find them.

The rest of the charges are a mixture of petty frauds and thefts but Fontaine's unique stamp is on some of them. For instance, in one of the car hire frauds – perpetrated at Hertz Rent-A-Car in Alexandra Parade in Glasgow and using the name Hindley – he gave his address as '18 The Rue St Homburg, Paris'. He had clearly tried to impress a no doubt indifferent receptionist by giving himself an urbane mantle, but what difference would it have made had he given an address in London or Lancashire?

And his expensive hotel and 'Rolls-Royce' fantasy, which recurred frequently, made a less than extravagant appearance in charge six:

On 19 October 1965 at the Royal British Hotel, 2 Princes Street, Edinburgh he obtained the hire of a motor car and the services of a chauffeur from Messrs Mackay Brothers, 31 Hanover Street, Edinburgh without paying and intending not to pay the cost thereof, amounting to £8, and did defraud Mackay Brothers thereof.

Charge five, of course, related to defrauding the Royal British Hotel itself, of board and lodging charges to the extent of £6:18s:9d. He also stole two rings from the hotel.

In November he snatched the tray of rings from a jeweller's in Paisley and in December 1965 he even went on to obtain a lesser version of 'The Full Monty' – in its original sense – at the Montague Burton's store in Dumbarton High Street, where he presented another dud cheque for a pair of trousers and a sheep-skin jacket.

Fontaine's combination of high society and low-life activities was extraordinary enough, but the indictment sets out crimes committed at a time when he should perhaps have been taking more care to evade arrest. The impulse to impersonate a man of means obviously took precedence over the need to stay one step ahead of the authorities, and there appeared to be no heed given to adopting a wiser lower profile. Enduring fantasy evidently prevailed over fear of recapture.

However, only part of Fontaine's 'fugitive' activities can be plotted from the dates of the indictment in Scotland running from 17 September 1965 to 4 December 1965, but as often with Fontaine, the reality was even more implausible. In the end, he need not have gone to the bother of making his memoirs so far-fetched when the truth itself was fantastic enough.

27

A BESPOKE FAMILY

Given that he was at large in Scotland for three months, the 1966 Edinburgh indictment discloses fairly concentrated, but low-level, criminal activity. Yet something else happened during that hectic time, something that if it lacked independent verification, could be easily dismissed as another of Fontaine's baseless musings.

He *did* actually meet the pregnant Irish girl from Drogheda – not Dublin – called Margaret, in a London hotel. She was alone in a strange country and was about to experience an even stranger episode with a bizarre character. Fontaine bought her a drink, listened to her tale of shame and then saw his opportunity – teaming up would be mutually beneficial. The day after they met, Fontaine found them work as domestic help and from then on they played the anxious couple awaiting the happy event.

Margaret was twenty years old and he was forty-one and the temporary arrangement suited them both. For her, there was companionship during a lonely time, as, in those days, she had had to leave Ireland after becoming pregnant to a married police officer. For Fontaine, she was the perfect cover, although his other verifiable activities suggest that discretion was low in his priorities.

When he introduced her to his mother and Wootton, he told them they had been married at London's Caxton Hall and that he was the child's father, which, even for him, was fairly unlikely as he had only escaped from a high security jail in September of that year, just over three months before the child was born. Margaret and he did spend some time as a 'live-in couple' at an address in Paddock Wood near Tunbridge Wells after Fontaine answered an advert using stolen stationery from top London hotels to have references written for him. Indeed, given Fontaine's poor spelling and writing, it has to be assumed that someone else wrote all of the false testimonials he presented to employers on his behalf. In any event, the new employer failed to check them, they got the job and duties were light.

It was no coincidence, it seems, that there was a spate of break-ins and thefts during their stay at Paddock Wood, although, as previously, Fontaine invented many of the exploits that supposedly occurred during their stay. His favourite exaggerations involved their 'landlady' Mrs Neilsen. He claimed that one day, when she wasn't about, he found her bank statements, which revealed that, contrary to the image she portrayed, she was actually very wealthy. In light of that knowledge, he deliberately drew her into a conversation about a bogus land deal he was in the process of setting up and like a moth to a flame, she sought his advice about investments. She started giving him cash to invest and he started giving her regular 'dividends' to keep her hooked in what's become known as a 'Ponzi scheme'.

Next, she happened to become a bit drunk on the whisky Fontaine was continually dispensing to her and she left the cottage forgetting to take a signed blank cheque with her. Knowing exactly how much she had in her account, he completed it for the sum of £12,350 and, timing it perfectly with the banking hours, he was able to uplift the cash and disappear.

In truth, 'Mrs Neilsen' had actually employed him and Margaret for a short time as live-in help. There seems to be little doubt that he did finance his life on the run with break-ins, frauds and thefts in all parts of Britain, but if there was any truth in the fraudulent scheme perpetrated on Mrs Neilsen, it would have been simplicity itself for the police to trace him by his movements, not least of all by checking where Caroline had been born.

He also boasted of the fiddle that he carried out on the local jeweller, just before he fled with Mrs Neilsen's cash. He had made a point of visiting the shop and looking at various expensive pieces without buying them. As it was near Christmas time, he lit the coal fire, placed bundles of cash round the house where they could easily be seen, then phoned the jeweller and asked if he would mind bringing the items he had been looking at in the shop round to his house that night. The jeweller agreed and on his arrival at Fontaine's house, he poured him a large festive drink which, together with the effects of the roaring fire, served to befuddle the shop owner who, by dint of the visible stacks of ready cash, believed he was in the presence of a man of means. It was now time for the trap to close.

Fontaine chose to buy all of the goods the jeweller had brought and he asked the unsuspecting shop manager if he preferred payment in cash or by cheque. Not wanting to appear rude, the hapless jeweller said he would take either and Fontaine then paid him with a dud cheque. As soon as the jeweller had gone, Fontaine packed up and left Paddock Wood forever.

Again, should such a crime have been committed, the victim seems to have made no complaint and Fontaine had happened to chance upon a jeweller whose business brain was easily stupefied, particularly as he had been given the option of cash.

Margaret however had a different account of their brief but eventful time together. To begin with, she had no idea that he was an escaped prisoner, although she said that he did eventually confess he was a fugitive. She said he only told her as much about himself 'as he wanted her to know'. The reason that no one got to know him was that he didn't know himself, she thought, and she quickly realised that it was almost impossible to be certain when he was telling the truth and when he was telling lies.

She had been impressed by him at first, but thought his attitude towards her 'strange' and, probably correctly, guessed he needed her to mask the fact he was a fugitive from justice. Contrary to Fontaine's warm self-assessment, she felt it had not been 'one of the world's great romances' and she was fully aware that his regular absences were due to his preference for the company of his own sex. Looking back, she considered that they had really just used each other and she had had no real feelings for him at all. She did however think that he had a genuine fondness for her daughter Caroline.

When the child was born on 18 December 1965, Fontaine seemed truly delighted and indeed may even have convinced himself that he actually was the father – until his death he called Caroline his daughter. He recalled buying flowers and champagne and, inevitably, hiring a Rolls-Royce to take the mother and child home, but, of course, none of that can be confirmed and neither Margaret herself nor staff at the home have any recollection of either presents for the new mother and daughter, or a prestige limousine appearing to take them home.

It's the mundane events that make the verifiable aspects of Fontaine's story so intriguing. Using the name 'Philips' – as in the 'Anne Philips' of his teenage years – he actually did register the birth, despite being on the run from prison. He informed the authorities that the mother was 'Margaret Fitzgerald' but did not provide a name for the child. The registrar, of course, just had to be a 'Mr Butler'.

Eighteen months later, by which time he was safely back in prison, Margaret – who temporarily *did* use the surname 'Fontaine' – registered the child's name as Caroline and at the same time, Fontaine's mother Marion applied to have her son's name removed from the register as the child's father. Margaret later emigrated to Canada where she married and settled down, leaving Caroline with the Woottons who officially adopted her and raised her as their daughter. Whilst Fontaine gave himself top marks in his romantic interlude with the smitten Margaret, she later revealed, ' . . . to tell the truth, I was very happy when he was recaptured.'

Just before his recapture, however, Fontaine arranged dinner for most of the family at a hotel – that his brother Donald was not invited would have later ramifications – and the evening was a success, with him and Margaret wearing expensive clothes and the pair of them staying in a room in the hotel. The following morning, however, Margaret awoke to find Fontaine had disappeared and Wootton was obliged to pay the bill, then transport Margaret and the baby to London where Fontaine had fled overnight. He explained to Margaret that he had had a feeling that he was in danger so had left without disturbing her.

As it turned out, Fontaine was right to be jumpy. He was eventually arrested when he and Margaret went for a brief stay in Weston-super-Mare. The puzzle for Fontaine was, having successfully evaded capture and taken so many outrageous risks, how did the police manage to track him there? The answer seems to be that Donald, perhaps bitter over his exclusion from the dinner party, had made a discreet phone call to the police, something that would have very serious consequences for *him* at a later date.

28

PUNISHING A WARDER – THE PARKHURST CASE

Fontaine's Version:

Corrupt warder who altered prison records for money; other prisoners speak up and warder is tried; defence contend that money not used in prison; Fontaine astounds court by producing banknote.

Fontaine was serving ten years' 'preventive detention' in Parkhurst top security jail when he discovered that the key for the greenhouse also opened the door to the prison's records office. Seeking to cause maximum trouble – and earn some money – Fontaine devised a plot against a prison officer he disliked called Harry Jackson.

Also in Parkhurst at the time was a Soviet spy called Morris Cohen. Cohen – or 'Peter Kroger' as he had been known – had been arrested along with his wife in 1961 for their involvement in the 'Portland Spy Ring', which had infiltrated the Royal Navy. The 'Krogers' had been posing as antiquarian book dealers and the attic in their house in Ruislip, Middlesex, was festooned with what nowadays would be seen as antiquarian spy equipment such as large transmitters and antennae.

Fontaine and another prisoner called Patrick 'Carson' discussed stealing Cohen's file and selling it to the newspapers, 'Carson' to smuggle it out whilst on a home visit. Using the greenhouse key, Fontaine took Cohen's file but Carson hesitated; knowing Fontaine well, he suspected that he was somehow trying to set him up, so he returned the file to him after he'd read it. Undeterred, Fontaine tried to interest the campaigning journalist Paul Foot at *Private Eye* and at that point, Carson realised Fontaine was serious so he relented and smuggled it out.

The concocted story involved prison officer Harry Jackson stealing prisoners' personal files, then letting them see the files for a fee. Fontaine claimed that Jackson offered Cohen's file to him for £30. Ostensibly filled with indignation at Jackson's outrageous breach of trust, Fontaine reported the matter to the Governor. Indeed, he claimed he had to visit him three times and resort to producing his own personal file before the Governor became interested and called in the police.

The simple truth was that when Fontaine was caught with the stolen papers, he blamed Jackson, and somehow the authorities took the case up and Jackson's trial for theft began in July 1968 at Winchester Crown Court.

The obvious weak point in the Crown case was the calibre of the prosecution witnesses; apart from Fontaine and Carson, there were ten other top security inmates. In the course of the evidence, some of Fontaine's prison jottings, including a reference to the wealthy philanthropist Sir Charles Clore, were put to him to try to demonstrate he was something of a fantasist. Ironically, Fontaine *had* actually worked for Clore, albeit only for a few days.

The other apparently sound defence tactic was to deride the suggestion that money to pay a corrupt warder was even attainable in a top security prison like Parkhurst.

This gave Fontaine his hoped-for opportunity. According to his biography, the detective who spoke to him in a side room in the court building just before Fontaine was due to give evidence, dropped a ten pound note as he left the room. Fontaine, who had already been searched that morning, picked it up and put it in his top pocket.

Whilst he undoubtedly produced a note in court – the

101

newspapers reporting it was only one pound – the tale has all the ingredients of Fontaine's implacable hatred of authority, the obvious implication being that the unscrupulous detective was either coaching Fontaine in his evidence and had dropped the note accidentally, or he had intentionally dropped the money to 'assist' the prosecution case. In any event, Fontaine certainly enjoyed the press attention the case attracted, including the headline: 'Jail man shows magic £1 note to jury'.

His triumphant tale ends with the curious judge examining the note closely and the court 'falling silent'. Yet despite the magical appearance of the banknote evidence – given Fontaine's lifelong habit of 'banking' paper money within his person, it's to be hoped that the judge washed his hands at the first adjournment – the jury correctly concluded he *was* an incorrigible liar and found Jackson not guilty. Fontaine was transferred to Hull Prison shortly thereafter, still smarting about the perceived 'injustice' of it all.

It might be expected that matters should be left at that, but the mind-set that concocts such a scheme, then sees it through with perjured evidence and the surprise production of the banknote, necessitates that there is no such thing as a lost cause. His anger at the verdict stemmed from him being completely incapable of seeing anything other than his own point of view, and he engaged the ever-obliging John Wootton to approach certain newspapers in an effort to keep the story running. By then, however, interest was dwindling, particularly as the truth about the greenhouse key had emerged towards the end of the trial, ensuring Jackson's acquittal. Wootton's ineffective attempts to sell his friend's fictitious version seems to be the first time Fontaine tried to use the press for his own purposes.

The 'Patrick Carson' who conjoined with Fontaine in the false allegation was another dangerous dreamer who was to come to public attention a few years later. Ludovic Kennedy's 1976 publication *A Presumption of Innocence – The Amazing Case of Patrick Meehan* was about 'Carson' under his real name. The book and his legal team's efforts were important in gaining Meehan a Royal Pardon following his conviction for the murder of Rachel Ross in Ayr, Scotland, in 1969.

Kennedy publicly cast doubt on some worrying irregularities in the police enquiry and Meehan's solicitor, Joe Beltrami, was able to reveal that two other villains had been the true culprits. Meehan received compensation from the authorities for the miscarriage of justice he had suffered, but if Kennedy – or any of the defence team who worked towards justice for their client – thought that Meehan might be grateful for their efforts, they were mistaken.

Suffering from a Fontaine-style delusion, Meehan decided it was time he became a player in world politics and took things a stage further by alleging in his eccentric book *Framed By MI5* that he had been convicted of the Ayr murder on the express instructions of British government agents, a claim based upon an unfounded belief in his importance in the world of international espionage.

Meehan had been in and out of prison in his early years due to his activities as a cracksman or safe-blower. Following an escape from Nottingham Prison in 1963, Meehan had fled to what was then East Germany where he unsuccessfully tried to persuade the authorities there that he could help 'spring' Soviet spies from British prisons. In particular, he claimed he could help free George Blake who had been sentenced to a whopping forty-two years for breaching the 1911 Official Secrets Act, after he had 'turned' in his role as an MI6 operative to become a double agent acting for the Soviets.

When Blake did actually escape from Wormwood Scrubs in 1966, however, it had nothing to do with Meehan. Blake swiftly made his way to Moscow where he lived the rest of his life convinced of the moral superiority of Marxist-Leninism and probably either unaware of, or unconcerned about, the existence of Patrick Meehan. Meehan's sojourn in the communist bloc ended ignominiously when the East Germans simply let him go, as they had quickly established that he was one of the ineffectual daydreamers anxious to become embroiled in the politics of the Cold War.

When Fontaine and Meehan met in Parkhurst in the 1960s, they already knew each other from previous jail sentences. Meehan mentioned Fontaine to Ludovic Kennedy as having a 'steady stream of society magazines' sent in to him. Meehan also revealed that his former wife destroyed the stolen files Fontaine had given him in Parkhurst, a common sense approach that neither man would have been capable of. He also told Kennedy that he could never fully trust Fontaine due to his vicious personality, citing Fontaine's boast that he once made an employer who had annoyed him 'very ill' by serving him toadstools instead of mushrooms. Meehan told the tale in 1979, by which time Fontaine was serving a 'natural life' sentence having been convicted of four murders, so Meehan's assessment was hardly a revelation. He summed it up by saying he wouldn't trust Fontaine 'as far as he could throw Buckingham Palace'.

Despite his wariness, it is no great surprise that Meehan and Fontaine were friends, of a sort, in prison. Both were Glaswegian core-criminals who craved notoriety and steadfastly refused to take responsibility for their own actions. Fontaine must surely have been envious of Meehan's pardon when it eventually came. After all, Paddy now had a degree of community sympathy, a compensatory payment from the public purse, and above all, a high-profile acknowledgement that, at least in one of his many crimes, he had been wrongly convicted. Fontaine too would have loved to be seen as a victim, but then, he was guilty of *all* the crimes he was charged with plus, if any of his claims are to be believed, many he never faced in court.

It is clear from Meehan's knowledge of Fontaine that he became increasingly adept at bending others to his will, not only through exploitive manipulation, but also by exuding a malicious psyche that intimidated even the hardest of criminals. Despite the fact that his tales of ingenious thefts and dazzling scams were patently exaggerated, one thing was for certain – he was not someone to be crossed.

29

EMBASSY EMBARRASSMENT – THE SOVIET CONSULATE AFFAIR

Fontaine's Version:

He comes into possession of important government papers; tries to use them to release Barnard; tries to interest the Soviets; sees Soviet official at Consulate; sees Soviet official in Hyde Park; Special Branch find papers and gun; strikes deal with prosecution; given light sentence in closed court.

Fontaine's three-year sentence in 1953 for the Mowbray House job was the last, bar two, of the relatively short terms of imprisonment he was to receive. Apart from a three-year sentence for burglary at Preston Crown Court in June 1975, he was given two years at Newington Causeway Crown Court in September 1973 for handling stolen property with a concurrent six months for unlawful possession of a firearm.

As he himself later contended, the latter sentence does seem lenient, as do the six months for possessing a firearm. His version of how that came to be might even contain a modicum of truth.

After being transferred to Hull Prison following the Parkhurst warder case, Fontaine met and purportedly fell in love with a tearaway called David Barnard. Barnard had been convicted at the Old Bailey in 1964 of shooting a Finsbury moneylender's clerk in the head with intent to rob him – with ten other charges of breaking and entering to be taken into account – and had received twelve years. The *Daily Express* reported that the judge,

Mr Justice Milmo, curiously commented that, 'It is no fault of yours [sic] that you are not standing in the dock charged with capital murder. Judges have to harden their hearts against people like you.' The court also heard that Barnard had been sent to Borstal in 1962 after admitting 177 cases of theft and housebreaking and that he described himself as a 'lone wolf'.

In 1967, when he was on the run from Wormwood Scrubs, a policeman, who was a veteran of the Arnhem debacle in World War Two, was awarded the George Medal when he cornered and disarmed Barnard as he threatened to shoot him and his colleagues.

In Fontaine's case, 'love' certainly worked in mysterious ways. Despite the discovery of this soulmate, after Fontaine was released on parole in 1972 – not in 1970 as he wrongly recorded in his biography – he inexplicably married Ruth Holmes. It was shortly after this marriage that he came into possession of the stolen briefcase and papers.

From the start, his fond recollection of an evening of marital accord in Ruth's flat prior to the phone ringing with the offer of the stolen items is highly improbable. He took the post at Grimshaw Hall in Warwickshire in order to avoid Ruth as he was no longer able to keep up the pretence of the love-struck spouse, which hadn't really lasted long anyway. The ever-trusting Hazel, just one of his many lovers at the time, had joined him at Grimshaw Hall where they were both employed.

The actions of 'the thief' appear to be very odd. Having stolen the briefcase, he was not only unable to figure out a way of opening it, but he then ran the risk of detection by hawking it round on the phone on the speculative basis that it might contain something valuable.

Those who knew Fontaine noted his constant absences due to his twin pursuits of housebreaking and homosexual encounters. It seems likely that he simply stole the briefcase himself but for some reason was reluctant to say so, probably as the real story did not match up to the shadowy world of intrigue he imagined himself to be inhabiting at the time of writing.

The *Guardian* for 11 August 1973 reported the case as 'Butler hid stolen Cabinet papers in wine store'. It reported the following:

> The documents were left by Mr R. S. Guinness – a First Secretary at the Foreign Office, on secondment to the Cabinet Office . . . in a briefcase in the hall of his home in Hereford Square, South Kensington, London.
>
> When he returned from a social engagement with his wife at 12.40am on June 15, the door was open and the briefcase had gone.

Given the proximity of Guinness's flat to Ruth's, it is probable that Fontaine actually broke in, having cased the place at some point when he had been visiting her.

However he obtained possession of the papers, Fontaine was just the sort to wildly overestimate their value. He probably did imagine himself as the astute negotiator holding a desperate establishment to account, but his total detachment from reality emerges when he considered, then acted upon, the idea of 'bartering' for his male lover's freedom with some obviously minor departmental documents. Underlining his own lack of insight, even Fontaine admitted that it only belatedly occurred to him that the prison authorities would be on to him as soon as he mentioned the prisoner's name. If that wasn't brainless enough, how could an approach to the Soviets possibly assist Barnard's early release?

There was something inevitable about his approach to the Soviet Consulate, as that was a fairly regular channel for the self-important but disaffected types who craved attention in those days. Most of them assumed their importance would be greatly enhanced overnight if they approached the perceived Cold War enemy and professed admiration for the communist system. The staff at Soviet embassies and consulates must have been used to – and privately amused by – the quite frequent callers who ultimately had little to offer but a secret desire to achieve instant notoriety or recognition. Unlike today, the Soviet threat became a focus for aggrieved characters who could dress up their real or imagined complaints as legitimate political points of principle.

The simple truth then appears to be that it was just another of his or a friend's break-ins that he embroidered with the usual spy fantasy – stock-in-trade surveillance photographs, masculine-looking Soviet women, shady contacts in the park and the inevitable book of matches from the Dorchester; an added 'James Bond' touch was the Special Branch already knowing his favourite tipple.

In reality, Fontaine actually went to the Soviet Consulate on four occasions but was never taken seriously; neither was there a walk in the park to counter MI5 surveillance during which a contact number was given out. The whole espionage scenario existed only in Fontaine's head and when he realised he was unable to 'trade' the papers he had, he simply hid them.

When the venture ended in failure, as the majority of Fontaine's criminal enterprises did, he confessed that he actually had no admiration for the communist system but was more inclined to being a monarchist, a fact, no doubt, which brought comfort and assurance to all at the Palace.

In its report on the court case, the *Guardian* described how the prosecuting counsel told the court that in view of the nature of the documents, careful consideration had been given to the matter and it was decided that no further charges were justified. The article concluded with the information that Fontaine had been 'jointly employed' at Grimshaw Hall with a woman who had been living with him, whilst his legal wife, Ruth, lived at an address in West Kensington and, despite what had happened, she was in court and was 'standing by him'. But rather than 'stand by him', Ruth seems to have pitied Fontaine, whom she quickly divorced after making the disastrous mistake of marrying him in the first place.

Apart from having to separate fact from fiction in one of Fontaine's yarns, the worth of the story lies in the legitimate point he makes himself. Not only had he been the subject of preventive detention before, but he had also been sentenced to *five years* for an analogous firearms offence.

Why *did* he receive such a light sentence?

And why did he serve his sentence in the then more relaxed regime of Long Lartin Prison?

Of course, the simple answer might be that – as government officials maintained at the time – the papers were of low status and of limited use to outsiders.

30

SEXUAL ADVENTURES – PART THREE: MARY, RUTH AND HAZEL

Ruth, however, was not the only woman to fall for Fontaine's amorous ruses during his spell of freedom in the early 1970s. Throughout this time he managed to charm his way into the arms of three different women.

His manipulative personality was of course on full display during his previous prison stretch as he had conspired – unsuccessfully – with others to set up Jackson, the Parkhurst warder, and had then been moved to Hull Prison. There he had met the first of his two male prison lovers – both Davids – 'the love of his life' Dave Barnard, who was to cause him 'much joy and, eventually, incredible heartbreak', and later in Long Lartin Prison, David Wright, the irresistible but amateur young thief who would be his first murder victim.

Fontaine's twenty months of liberty were particularly hectic and he appears to have packed in as much activity as he could, possibly in the certain knowledge that his freedom would soon be curtailed.

A condition of his release in early 1972 was that he had to live in the prison hostel in Preston, Lancashire, for eight months and to work in Whittingham Psychiatric Hospital at Goosnargh near the town. Whether this was an appropriate work assignment for a mentally unstable criminal was never to be determined; it is likely that while working at the hospital he stole the chloroform which he was to employ with deadly effect in

110

the murder of his brother Donald six years later, the first murder by that means in British criminal history.

He mentions meeting – and according to Fontaine, having sex with – one of the women who worked there, Mary Coggle, on his first day at work. She was separated from her husband, seemed to have little or no contact with her eight children and apparently supplemented her income by part-time prostitution and selling stolen goods, particularly stolen cheque books and driving licences. Mary was small time, pliable and ultimately dispensable, as just short of six years after he met her, Fontaine was to murder her as well.

During that unusually long period of freedom, Fontaine also met Hazel and Ruth, both of whom called themselves 'Fontaine' in the belief they had the right to do so, although only one of them had the legal entitlement.

Hazel Patterson owned a newsagent's shop near to the hostel and Fontaine, of course, later claimed to have been in the highly unlikely role of being her security adviser, when he gave her good advice about how to stop the shop takings diminishing. Hazel later told her story to the press, and the difference between their respective perceptions is testament to how Fontaine had the ability to deceive otherwise shrewd female companions.

She met him one day in June 1972 when he came into her shop and they soon started dating. After about a month, she found out that he was in the process of completing a sentence of 'fifteen years'. After they talked about it, she told him it made no difference to how she felt about him, and anyway he had told her his version of what had led to his conviction and he had vowed he would never again go back to prison. She thought he deserved another chance with life and told a reporter: 'He said, "That's what I hoped you'd say. That's what I expected you to say." Then we made passionate love for the rest of the night. I knew then that I'd fallen in love with him.'

Lovemaking with perfumed baths thereafter was a daily occurrence for some weeks and Hazel thought they were married 'in spirit'. He gave her a ring and told her never to take it off, then he moved in with her and told her daughter he would always look after her mother. Amidst strong rumours of actual matrimony, neighbours threw rice over the couple as they left for a weekend away and when they returned Hazel sent cake to relatives.

Eventually, Hazel realised that they never seemed to be alone together and that his visitors were always male. She also began to notice that their passionate love life was rapidly cooling. One weekend he gave her flowers and a present for her birthday but told her that as he had to go to London on business they would celebrate when he got back. She was later to realise that that was when he met Ruth. He often did not even bother to go to London but would meet Ruth off the London train. He then married her in September 1972, as Hazel said, 'just round the corner' from her shop in Preston.

What made him get married, and do so in Preston?

Ruth had a flat and a job in London, but he insisted on a civil ceremony in Lancashire, presumably as he got a thrill from controlling the event and from the prospect of Hazel finding out.

Naturally, he falsified his age and address for the marriage certificate and Ruth was later quoted in a newspaper as saying:

He was marvellous company and we went to all the best places – drinks at the Dorchester and dinner at the Café Royal. Nothing sexual happened before our marriage, but then nothing happened after it either. Then one night, to my joy, it suddenly did happen. I was so happy.

But when we were making love, he called me a man's name, 'Oh, Davie, Oh, Davie,' he said. I froze. It was the worst thing that could happen to a woman. I said quite coldly, 'My name's Ruth, not Davie.' Then he told me Davie was his homosexual lover.

Unsurprisingly, the marriage did not last long and he was soon back with Hazel, again promising marriage but in reality

MURDER ARCHIBALD HALL

TUESDAY May 3 1978

Daily Record

8p   SCOTLAND'S BIGGEST DAILY SALE   No. DG,712

BLOODLUST OF THE BUTLER

THIS was the portrait of Archibald Hall as his upper-class masters knew him . . . the silver-tongued butler always at their beck and call.

But at the High Court in Edinburgh yesterday, Hall's other face was revealed—the Glasgow hoodlum turned conman, the homosexual who became a cold killer.

Hall and his friend, Michael Kitto, smiled and joked as they were sentenced to life for the murder of wealthy ex-M P Walter Scott-Elliot last December.

The ex-butler was also sentenced for the killing of small-time crook David Wright.

And both men may face further proceedings in England.

PORTRAIT OF A KILLER
Hall in his butler pose: Suave, impeccable . . . and a psychopathic killer.

● Smiles end trail of death—Page 2
● Crazy con man becomes killer—Pages 16 and 17
● From Glasgow tearaway to Belgravia butler—Pages 18 and 19

Front cover of *Daily Record* from May 1978 following Fontaine's appearance at Edinburgh High Court where he pleaded guilty to charges of murdering Walter Travers Scott-Elliot and David Wright.

A young Archibald Hall with sister Violet in 1931. She was to remain loyal to him throughout his criminal career and even after he pleaded guilty to murdering their brother Donald.

The sign, which can still be seen today, showing the original name of the street where he was born.

The address in Partick, Glasgow, adjacent to Partick Bowling Club, where Archibald Thomson Hall was born in July 1924.

The address at Cranworth Street in Glasgow's West End where the Hall family returned to after they left Catterick in disgrace in 1940. Contrary to certain press reports, the Hall family were not brought up in the by now clichéd 'mean streets' of the city.

Joan Fontaine, star of the 1940 Alfred Hitchcock film *Rebecca*, which had such an effect on the young Archibald Hall that he began using the surname 'Fontaine'.

David Niven, the dashing lead of the 1939 version of the film *Raffles*. Fontaine seems to have incorporated some aspects of the film's plot into his biography in an effort to justify and glamourise his compulsive dishonesty.

Fontaine seen second from the left in the back row at a social event in Torquay held by the town Mayor in 1953 when he and John Wootton were on the run after the theft of jewels from Edinburgh's Mowbray House.

© MIRRORPIX.COM

John Wootton, Fontaine and his 'daughter' Caroline following his release from prison in 1972. On that occasion, he was at liberty for an unusually long eighteen months, during which time he not only moved in with Hazel Patterson but also married Ruth Holmes.

© MIRRORPIX.COM

© MIRRORPIX.COM

Donald Hall, Fontaine's ill-fated younger brother, pictured during his stint of National Service. After being discharged from the army, he became a petty criminal and an object of hatred to his older brother who harboured dreams of wealth through well-planned robberies.

Hazel Patterson, the Preston shopkeeper who lived to regret falling in love with Fontaine after they met in 1972. Her son gained a measure of revenge when he later traced Fontaine to the butler's post at Kirtleton Estate, Dumfriesshire, and alerted the police.

David Michael Wright, the small time thief Fontaine met in prison. He became Fontaine's first known murder victim when he shot him in 1977, then buried the body near to Kirtleton Estate. He later claimed Wright was blackmailing him.

Lady Margaret 'Peggy' Hudson who employed Fontaine in 1977 after paying a fee to an agency which found her a new 'butler'. Fontaine was arrested and charged with five murders before he could carry out his plan to rob her.

The police searching the Kirtleton Estate grounds for the body of David Wright in January 1978.

© MIRRORPIX.COM

The area in Inverness-shire off the Tomich to Cougie Road, where Walter Travers Scott-Elliot (inset) was driven to, then murdered. Both he and his wife were to die within six weeks of employing Fontaine.

Walter Travers Scott-Elliot.

Michael John Kitto as a young man. After being introduced to Fontaine by Mary Coggle in 1977, Kitto went from being a social nuisance to a triple murderer in the space of two months.

© MIRRORPIX.COM

What used to be known as Middle Farm Cottage in Newton Arlosh, Cumbria. Fontaine rented the cottage in October 1977, two weeks after leaving his post at Kirtleton. It was the scene of the murders of Mary Coggle in December 1977 and Donald Hall in January 1978.

The Joiners' Arms, Newton Arlosh. Fontaine, Kitto and Coggle drank there before and after murdering Walter Travers Scott-Elliot and before Coggle herself was murdered by the other two.

Mary Coggle.

© MIRRORPIX.COM

The bridge over the Black Burn at Middlebie, Dumfriesshire where the body of Mary Coggle (inset) was dumped just before Christmas 1977. She was found lying in the stream near to where the debris can be seen in the middle of the picture.

Fontaine being escorted into Haddington Sheriff Court in January 1978 on his first appearance, following the discovery of Donald Hall's body in a car boot.

Fontaine being transported in custody after his attempted suicide in January 1978.

sponging off a willing victim. Fontaine said that when she sold her shop she used some of the proceeds to buy him a Jaguar car, but he also told his sister Violet he'd bought it himself. Whatever the case, Hazel was an eager listener to his tales of robbing rich aristocrats to assist hard-up friends and of sex-starved lady employers who only wanted him for his body. She had completely fallen for him and, incredibly, their relationship lasted – with breaks – until he was jailed for his natural life in 1978. Maybe Hazel can be forgiven for being so foolish as she had some reason to think him genuine; in the course of their time together he was said to have written over 400 'love' letters to her.

Limited vengeance – on her behalf – was to come.

Hazel's son, stung by Fontaine's treatment of his mother, successfully traced and ousted Fontaine from his post with Lady Hudson three years later at Kirtleton House in the Scottish Borders, an action which probably saved her life.

31

THE FIRST MURDER –
DAVID MICHAEL WRIGHT

THE SCENE IS SET

In January 1977, Fontaine was released from a three-year sentence imposed at Preston Crown Court in 1975 for burglary and car theft and was eager to seek new victims. Living mostly on her own and in her seventies, Lady Hudson of Kirtleton was just the sort Fontaine liked to prey upon.

Lady Hudson paid £20 per week for a butler, his bed and board included; she had even paid an agency £140 for the privilege of sourcing Fontaine but history fails to record whether she later claimed a refund. She was rightly careful about the new man and as well as hiring him through the agency, she also explained that she would have to do more than rely on the written references Fontaine supplied. Accordingly, she took the precaution of telephoning and speaking to a 'Major Wootton' who answered all her questions and concluded by telling her he was sorry to lose him. The number supplied for the 'Major' was a public box beside John Wootton's house in Lytham St Anne's, but it may have been that Fontaine himself answered the call.

When she picked Fontaine up from the train station at Carlisle on 31 May 1977, she obviously had no idea of the genuine danger she was in, particularly considering part of the 'butler' package, which is a common feature of country estates, included access to shotguns. Increasingly frustrated in his efforts to hit the jackpot, Fontaine had become desperate and there seems little

114

doubt he was planning theft or robbery from the start of his employment there. After his background was exposed and the police escorted him from the premises ninety-two days later, he was determined to take revenge against Lady Hudson, based, in his twisted mind, on the fact that she had somehow managed to escape his predations. His subsequent let of a cottage at Newton Arlosh in Cumbria, only thirty-two miles from Kirtleton, clearly suggested an intended future attack.

But despite his unfulfilled plans for Lady Hudson, he had managed to get away with one major crime at Kirtleton. He had murdered for the first time.

Fontaine's 'final versions' of all the murders are, presumably, what he wanted the rest of the world to believe – image being more important to him than the truth – and what has come to be accepted in the murder of Wright is probably the furthest from reality. His 'final version' had Wright drunkenly aiming a shot at him as he sat up in bed because Fontaine refused to rob Lady Hudson and ended with Fontaine turning the tables on him at the rabbit hunt.

Wright was a small-time crook born in Birmingham who had convictions for assault, theft, burglary and assault with intent to rob. When he failed to appear at Birmingham Crown Court on 14 July 1977 to face a charge of aggravated burglary, a warrant was taken for his arrest, but by that time he was probably in a makeshift tomb at the quaintly named Pokeskine Sike Burn on the Kirtleton Estate.

According to Fontaine – who was twenty-one years older than Wright – the two had met in Long Lartin Prison in Worcestershire where a sexual bond developed between them. Their friendship and sex life progressed but Fontaine became resentful when Wright failed to get in touch with him or acknowledge the inside information he gave him about Grimshaw Hall.

Regardless of that slight, when Wootton told Fontaine that Wright had been trying to get in touch with him, Fontaine called him and invited him to Kirtleton, solely, he claimed, so he could have sex with him. When Wright arrived, he told Fontaine that he needed to lie low for a while as he had been involved in a 'mugging gone wrong' and had killed a Pakistani man in a gents' toilet.

Things started to go downhill when Wright ran up large debts with the local bookie, which Fontaine felt obliged to pay. On a more sinister note, Fontaine claimed that Wright was impatient to steal from Lady Hudson, but he forbade it, not on moral grounds, obviously, but because it should be done after Fontaine was no longer employed there. Disregarding his wishes, Wright took a ring, which Fontaine then found in Wright's room wrapped in a sock. Yet, despite these mounting grievances, Fontaine let the younger man stay.

'Letting him stay' led to Fontaine pleading guilty at Edinburgh High Court on 2 May 1978 to murdering Wright on a date between 1 July and 30 November 1977 by repeatedly shooting him in a field adjoining the Pokeskine Sike Burn.

In the circumstances, a denial would have been difficult.

He had been apprehended, initially, on the other murder charges he was to face, but then simply volunteered that he had killed Wright and took the police to the gravesite. Had he not, it's doubtful that Wright's body would have been discovered, at least during the currency of Fontaine's lifetime.

Following his arrest in January 1978, Fontaine gave details about Wright's murder in the voluntary statement he gave to police in his own peculiar spelling, punctuation and handwriting.

Reproduced here, it reads:

He Had tRied to shoot me in Bed at her House Previous evening Bullet when into centre Panel of Bed and wall. I Have filled same with Poly filler. He is buried Near Her estate on Forestry Commission Land I am Prepared to show Police exact spot where He is. I removed most items of identification from his body and flung them away. This Happened while Lady Hudson was away in London with Mrs Loydd when they returned I told them I Had seen

Wright leave to take up a JOB IN TORQUAY, they believed it.

Essentially, the story was the same one he later recounted in book form – the deceased man had first attempted to kill him. In *The Prison Cell Confessions of Archibald Thompson Hall* from 1981, he explained that whilst he had fallen in love with Dave Barnard, he 'looked favourably' on David Wright, which is an important difference from the later tale and possibly hints at the real motive for the murder.

The earlier version had Fontaine corresponding with Wright who then asked if he could visit Fontaine for a holiday. Lady Hudson had been told of the suggestion and she agreed to let Wright help out around the estate, without him being officially employed. Fontaine's rekindling of the relationship with Wright was 'just what he needed' at the time, he wrote, but he was soon to discover a 'new and frightening side' to his erstwhile lover.

Shortly after he arrived, Wright apparently confessed to picking up a rich, gay Pakistani man in a Birmingham night-club, before killing him and leaving the body in an alley. At the time, Fontaine realised Wright was referring to the 1976 death of Ramji Fatania who had been found in the street dying from injuries so severe it was thought they could have been caused by being struck by a car. This unsettling information caused Fontaine to be frightened of the younger, fitter man and he became 'extremely nervous' of him and worried for his own safety.

Wright thereafter began to 'bleed him white' and tension esca-lated when Fontaine realised that Lady Hudson's diamond ring was missing. He searched Wright's room for it, to no avail, but in so doing he chanced upon a girl's name – 'Annette' – and her telephone number in nearby Dumfries. Intuitively, he knew she would have the missing ring, so he dialled the number, successfully impersonated Wright and when she confirmed she still had the 'present' she had been given, he arranged to meet her in the County Hotel. On his arrival, he was able to spot Annette straight away as she was wearing the stolen ring, and when he approached her and explained the true situation, she immediately gave it back to him, commenting that Wright had dropped hints that he was Lady Hudson's grandson. They talked for a while and she told him she was a nurse.

Within two years of the events described, the compiler of *The Prison Cell Confessions of Archibald Thompson Hall*, James Copeland, investigated the strange account of how Fontaine had retrieved the valuable ring and he was unable to trace any nurse called Annette. He did however trace a girl called Alice who had been going out with Wright. Alice told Copeland that she had never received any ring from Wright but mentioned that she had met both Wright and Fontaine on at least two occasions and remembered, significantly, that Fontaine clearly dominated the younger man.

The circumstances of Wright's attempted murder of Fontaine were to change, as well, when Fontaine recounted events to Copeland. There was no exhortation to 'rob' the house that night, just a 'strangled cry' from Wright who then fired at a fully awake Fontaine, but the cartridge hit the bed's headboard and the wall behind it. A struggle then ensued and Wright hit Fontaine on the face with the gun, but when Wright saw Fontaine's injury he started crying and dropped the weapon. Fontaine then seized the initiative and *ordered* Wright to fetch some towels to staunch the flow of blood and to clean up the bedclothes. Wright immediately obeyed.

They both bandaged Fontaine's injury then cleaned up the bed before Fontaine patched up the damage to the headboard and the wall using Polyfilla and brown boot polish. All the while, Wright begged forgiveness but Fontaine calmed him down and sent him to bed where within minutes the remorseful and confused drunk was fast asleep.

Realising how close he was to being killed, Fontaine suddenly experienced shock and phoned his sister Violet in Newcastle-under-Lyme. Violet later corroborated this phone call, describing how he was extremely upset and babbling on about how 'they tried to kill him' and that he had been hit on the face with a gun, but she also mentioned he said that he had had to lock himself in the study where the gun rack was. Violet later berated herself for not persuading Fontaine to leave Kirtleton that night, as she felt she could have stopped him from committing the first murder of his killing spree. But, judging from the results of a more in-depth examination of the murder, there was nothing she could have done, as by that time, Fontaine was determined to get rid of Wright – if he hadn't in fact done so already.

Fontaine told Copeland that after the shooting incident with Wright, he poured himself a brandy and weighed up the situation. On the one hand, Wright might make another attempt on his life and guns were easily to hand, but on the other, why should he 'be driven out by a bastard like Wright'? So he decided to get the decisive blow in the next morning. Accordingly, he and Wright – this time no mention of the usually omnipresent Wootton – set off, Fontaine counting Wright's cartridges as six this time. After four shots, Wright asked him why he wasn't shooting and he told him he didn't shoot baby rabbits. Just at that, two appeared, and Wright fired both of his remaining cartridges, hitting one of them. Fontaine suggested that they sit beside the burn for a smoke and, trustingly, Wright agreed, then sat down and lit a cigarette with his gold Dunhill lighter.

The chance Fontaine had been waiting for had presented itself. He shot Wright in the back of the head and then a further twice in the torso, but as he still showed signs of life, he fired another shot into Wright's twitching body then dragged it into the nearby ferns. After that he picked up the guns and Wright's cigarettes and lighter and went back to Kirtleton House where he locked the guns back in the rack.

Checking the wine cellar, he noticed that four bottles of champagne were missing, obviously consumed by Wright the night before, so he drove into town and bought four bottles of a different vintage to replace them in the cellar before Lady Hudson and her companion Mrs Lloyd returned from London. After a wash and change of clothes, he drove to the station to pick the ladies up and explained his facial injury as having been caused by a slip on exiting the swimming pool. He told them Wright had been offered, and accepted, a good job in Torquay. Lady Hudson, however, discovered the replacement champagne that night and Fontaine had to confess he had bought the bottles to replace the ones Wright had drunk, as he had been Fontaine's guest.

Later that night he went back to the murder site and tried to gouge a shallow grave with his hands, all the time crying and asking why Wright had made him do it, but he had to come back later in the night with a spade to dig properly then rush back to serve the ladies' breakfast.

He concluded this second version with the observation that he had no worries about Wright's disappearance sparking off an enquiry, as, although he had been married twice, he was a drifter who shunned contact with his family. Fontaine knew there was little chance of anxious questions from worried relatives, so he dismissed him from his mind – aside from one keepsake: Wright's classy gold Dunhill lighter.

WHAT REALLY HAPPENED?

When a suspect in a 'crime scene' programme or an accused in a real life trial has been seen to change their story, even by the smallest detail, the fact is latched upon as significant. Truth, after all, is unchangeable – or so the theory goes.

Clearly, both of Fontaine's stories cannot be accurate. Perhaps neither is.

What is certain is that he knew where Wright's body was and that on the day he picked his employer and her friend up from the station, he had obvious facial injuries, he said from slipping when leaving the 'outdoor' pool, which was actually indoors. He furthermore told them Wright, who was never seen alive again, had left for Torquay. Lady Hudson also confirmed that she discovered that four bottles of her usual champagne had been replaced by four of a different vintage.

Police later found damage to the wall in the bedroom Fontaine used in the house, which was consistent with a bullet being fired into it, and if Violet's recollection of the desperate call Fontaine made to her is accurate, it would fit in, time-wise at least.

Beyond that, however, not too much credence can be given to anything else Fontaine claimed about the circumstances of Wright's death.

For instance, we only have Fontaine's word that Wright was bisexual – or, if he was, that he was having a sexual relationship with Fontaine. There's nothing to show Wright burgled Grimshaw Hall or that he was involved in the murder of the man in Birmingham in 1976. Indeed, an inquest that year concluded that no cause of death could be established for the deceased.

Obvious discrepancies appear where the 'disappearance' of the diamond ring is mentioned – was it in Wright's sock or on 'Annette's' finger? Anyway, how could Fontaine know that a particular piece of jewellery was missing, rather than, say, being cleaned or valued or worn at the time?

Did Wright deliver the monologue ascribed to him when he had Fontaine at gunpoint in the bedroom, about 'robbing' the place that night, or did he simply give out 'a strangled cry'?

In a wider context, why was Fontaine so threatened by Wright's drunken rants? What would it matter to Fontaine if his past, yet again, caught up with him? His stated intention was to learn all he could about the layout and security at Kirtleton before leaving the post and returning at a later date to break in. Even if he did feel Wright was rushing him, how could the tension have escalated to the point of attempted murder? And if Wright's threats were purely a drunken mistake, Fontaine's homicidal retribution does seem something of an over-reaction.

On top of that, the number of cartridges Wright used up varies, as do the accounts of his shooting. Did Fontaine treat Wright to a full explanation of why he found it necessary to kill him, or did he sneak up behind him and shoot him in the head? And was Wootton present at the murder or not?

How could the ground be 'too frozen' to dig if the murder happened in July and where did the convenient spade appear from?

Ignoring Fontaine's sinister reputation, how could Wright be so stupid that he did not sense any danger as he unthinkingly joined a shooting party with the person he had tried to shoot the night before, particularly if it was just the two of them? Once the party headed off, Wright would surely have had to wonder why Fontaine seemed strangely inactive and reluctant to fire any shots.

The importance of establishing the manner of Wright's death lies in Fontaine's assertion that had he not committed the crime, he would not have gone on to kill, or be involved in the deaths of, four others. His justification for shooting Wright seems to be threefold: Wright had threatened to blackmail him, he had attempted to shoot him and he had broken a tacit criminal code by not acknowledging his debt to Fontaine for information supplied, none of which can be verified.

The 1978 Edinburgh indictment narrated that the locus of Wright's murder was 'a field adjoining the burn', but even though the prosecution was prepared to accept that aspect of the crime, there have to be misgivings about the true locus of the shooting, and hence the proper motive for the murder. Should it be considered, for instance, that Wright had *not* appeared in Fontaine's bedroom in a drunken homicidal rage and tried to shoot him as he lay peaceably in bed, then questions are raised as to the real reason for Wright's murder.

In that regard, investigating officers noted the following:

1. The mattress in Fontaine's bedroom had smears of human blood on one side but was heavily contaminated on the other.

2. The mattress cover had a large bloodstain at one corner,

a smaller one at the other and smears at the centre and the edge and that none of these corresponded with the stains on the mattress.

3. A hole 9" x 6.5" had been cut in the bed quilt and adjacent to it, and on other places on it there were burn and scorch marks.

4. The blood mentioned in headings 1 and 2 above could have come from *David Michael Wright*.

Adding that information to the starting premise that Fontaine was an incurable liar, it may paint an entirely different picture.

For instance, did he kill Wright on the bed and then move the body to the area of the stream for disposal? Was he able to drag the body there by himself or was the inclusion of Wootton in one version of the murder a clue to the fact that, in his usual complicit role, he arrived and helped Fontaine with the burial? Were Wootton's professed 'congratulations' to Fontaine for committing the 'perfect murder' a typical Fontaine false trail to deflect attention from the fact that Wootton was present at the murder?

When Fontaine took police to the body on 21 January 1978, it might be expected that he would follow the same route he and Wright allegedly followed from Kirtleton House on their rabbit hunting expedition. Instead, he directed them past the driveway to the house further north along the B722, before getting them to turn east along the B7068 towards Lockerbie, then immediately turn south onto a Forestry Commission track adjacent to the estate. In effect, he came to the grave from the opposite direction from that which might have been anticipated. At that time, vehicle access to within a few hundred yards of the burial site was possible, probably indicating that the body was moved from Fontaine's bedroom to the boot of a car before disposal, a feature of three of the four subsequent killings Fontaine was involved in.

He also said in his voluntary statement that Wright was 'buried *near* her estate on Forestry Commission land' rather than on Lady Hudson's estate where the 'rabbit shoot' took place.

It was probably also significant that he recalled how, as he and Kitto circled the Kirtleton Estate with Mary Coggle's body in the boot of their hired car a few months later on 18 December 1977, he thought about interring her beside Wright's corpse but changed his mind as Forestry Commission workers were on the lookout for 'Christmas tree thieves' at that time of year.

He was obviously aware that vehicle access could be gained to within a reasonable distance of the burial site through Forestry land.

Another, less probable, scenario would be that Wright was wounded in the bedroom and was hunted down as he fled from the house into the surrounding countryside where he was subsequently buried.

Whatever actually occurred, Fontaine evidently saw more glamour in the version so eagerly espoused by the press and crime journals at the time. Indeed, he need not have even told the authorities about Wright's murder and the prosecution was probably content to be circumspect about its surrounding circumstances, as he faced further murder charges in Edinburgh and later that year at the Old Bailey. It can thus be assumed that Fontaine used this opportunity to create the most flattering version of events possible, and thus that furthest from the truth.

The obvious reason for altering the circumstances and location of the killing would be to try to obscure the motive. One revelation that could shed light on Fontaine's actions lies in the true nature of the final weeks of his relationship with David Barnard. When Barnard was released from Hull Prison in 1974, he actually seems to have completely ignored Fontaine, who was far more adept at dishing out rejection than accepting it. Barnard, it appears, chose to simply go his own way after his release on parole, suggesting that Fontaine's tear-jerking scenario of his lover's tragic death at the wheel of the Jaguar has little or no proximity to the truth. The rejection by Barnard would also negate Fontaine's previous claim that it was the loss of his cherished lover that numbed him to all appreciation of human life, effectually creating the murderer and casting Fontaine as the innocent victim of fate's cruelty.

It might be that having already been snubbed by Barnard, Fontaine became unbearably jealous when it appeared that Wright was also rebuffing him by forming a relationship with a local girl, and in his dominant role, he decided that killing Wright would satisfy his ego. A lovers' tiff in the bedroom could have led to Fontaine struggling with the younger man before he broke free, unlocked the gun rack and returned to shoot him. In that event, the phone call to Violet would make some sense. Fontaine, whilst in a state of shock, mentioned 'having to lock himself in the study where the gun rack was' after some sort of fight, and that could have led to him arming himself and returning to his bedroom to finally settle the matter.

In that regard, his retention of Wright's Dunhill lighter might be seen as the typical psychopathic 'trophy', kept to remind the killer of the warm glow that thoughts of the killing occasioned.

There are certainly many questions that remain unanswered in relation to the murder of David Wright. Unfortunately, the true details will never be known since they were unnecessary in convicting the confessed murderer. However, despite being unable to resolve any of the glaring contradictions present in Fontaine's accounts of his first killing, it remains useful in underlining, once again, the lack of trust that can be placed in his 'stories', which really only serve to illustrate how he still tried to manipulate the truth even after receiving a 'genuine' life sentence. And of course, should sufficient doubt be cast on Fontaine's carefully crafted explanation for murdering Wright, his professed reasoning for the later killings can be totally undermined.

32

THE SPREE BEGINS –
DOROTHY SCOTT-ELLIOT

A SINISTER APPOINTMENT

When Hazel Patterson's son, Colin, made the telephone calls which led to Fontaine being escorted by police from Kirtleton Estate on 7 September 1977, he had the satisfaction of knowing that he had at least inconvenienced the man who had soaked so much money from his mother and ultimately broken her heart. He didn't know it at the time, but he may have also stopped Lady Hudson from being robbed, although she herself had begun to have serious worries about Fontaine and had arranged an appointment with the police to see if they knew anything about him. Colin also bore a purely personal grudge; Fontaine had sexually molested him when he was staying with his mother.

Fontaine, however, was to rent Middle Farm Cottage at Newton Arlosh in Cumbria near to Kirtleton five weeks later, using the name 'Robin Thompson' – 'Robin' being his and Kitto's shorthand for their stock in trade – and it's to be safely assumed Lady Hudson had been filed under 'unfinished business'.

Now back on the 'domestic' market and increasingly impulsive and unpredictable, Fontaine had again obtained forged references and taken a post with the Scott-Elliots in their fashionable Chelsea flat starting on 1 November 1977. The post included a live-in flat so the renting of the Cumbrian cottage *after* the position with the Scott-Elliots was secured could only have had one obvious purpose.

Firstly, he would deal with his new employers; within six weeks of Fontaine's appointment, both of the Scott-Elliots would be murdered and their bodies discarded in rural Scotland.

The first to die was the lady of the house.

Dorothy Alice Nunn or Scott-Elliot was twenty-two years younger than her husband, whom she had married in 1948, the year of his divorce from his first wife. She was the wealthy daughter of a Calcutta merchant and she had met her husband when he was managing director of The Bombay Company. They spent their days collecting antiques and occasionally travelling abroad. By late 1977, she was suffering badly from crippling arthritis and had signs of early senility.

According to Fontaine in *A Perfect Gentleman*, he was showing Kitto around the Scott-Elliot house, thinking Mrs Scott-Elliot was away till the following day. However, when the lady of the house unexpectedly appeared from her bedroom, Kitto reacted by clamping his hand over her mouth, whereupon she slumped to the ground. The murder, it seems, had been a tragic accident with Mrs Scott-Elliot's death a puzzling result of her being mildly constrained.

Not surprisingly, Fontaine's previous explanation for the murder differed from the later one in several respects. That time, he said he had given Mr Scott-Elliot a tranquiliser after he had served him dinner in bed and he had heard Mrs Scott-Elliot go to her bed after she had been on the phone to her niece.

The coast was now clear for Kitto to come in and discuss their plans for stealing as much as they could from the frail old couple. They had been drinking heavily and when Fontaine realised that they had run out of drink, he decided not to go out to buy some more, but to simply purloin it from the Scott-Elliots' healthy stock in the wine cellar. He made his way there, as did Kitto for reasons best known to himself, and as they passed Mrs Scott-Elliot's room, she unexpectedly appeared at the door and asked him what he was doing there and who was with him.

Kitto then sprang forward and clamped his hand over her nose and mouth before dragging her into the bedroom and suggesting they tie her up. When Kitto took his hand away from her face, though, there were smears of blood on it and she fell to the floor. Fontaine then took a pillow from the bed and, seizing an end each, they both pressed it against her face until she was no longer breathing. They then put her into bed and covered her up when they were convinced she was no longer alive.

Mr Scott-Elliot then appeared from his room enquiring about the commotion, but Fontaine assured him there was nothing amiss and that he had probably had a dream, so he gave him another sleeping tablet and the old gent went back to bed.

In that version then, Kitto had aimlessly followed Fontaine as he went to the cellar to replenish their drinks, and when he attacked Mrs Scott-Elliot she only collapsed and then they both smothered her to death.

The two men then cleaned up the bloodstains in the bedroom before retiring upstairs where Fontaine quickly fell into a deep sleep on the couch, but the worried Kitto stayed awake all night. When Fontaine awoke in the morning, he allayed Kitto's fears by telling him of the plan he had come up with after the previous night's events. Mary Coggle was to pose as the murdered woman and they were to go ahead with their plan to milk the Scott-Elliots' financial accounts dry.

With that, he served Mr Scott-Elliot's breakfast to him, which included tea laced with valium. As he did so, he told the old man that his wife had already gone to Scotland with a lady friend, but she wanted them to follow by car; she had suggested her husband dine in his club as his bags were being packed.

Mary having joined them, Fontaine told her and Kitto that their best plan was to take the body to Scotland, mainly because they had a better chance of acquittal in a Scottish rather than an English court due to the existence of the 'Not Proven' verdict there. They hired a car with Fontaine posing as Mrs Scott-Elliot's godson 'Roy Thompson', Kitto pretending he was the chauffeur and Mary the lady of the house. A hitch occurred when

Kitto gave his real date of birth rather than the one from the stolen driving licence he had proffered, but he rectified matters after the car hire clerk queried it.

The three of them then bought clothes in Harrods using pre-signed Scott-Elliot cheques, although Mary was already decked out in an expensive dress and fur coat belonging to the murdered woman.

The body was moved to the boot of the hired car and they set off for Scotland with Kitto driving the three others, including the sedated Mr Scott-Elliot, north. They stayed at Newton Arlosh for the night before dumping the body near Comrie in Perthshire and returning to Cumbria.

UNTESTED IN COURT

When Fontaine and Kitto appeared at the Old Bailey on 2 November 1978, the prosecution accepted Kitto's plea of guilty to the manslaughter of Mrs Scott-Elliot and Fontaine's plea of not guilty. It was explained that, as Fontaine had pleaded guilty to the murder of his brother Donald, the pleas tendered were accepted in order to save the public purse, and although not mentioned directly, by that time they were both serving life sentences from their appearance at Edinburgh High Court a few months earlier.

Addressing the court in mitigation on Kitto's behalf, John Mortimer QC – the creator of *Rumpole of the Bailey* – proved to be just as unmindful of political rectitude as his famous creation when he pointed out that his client had been the 'passive' partner in the homosexual bond he had formed with his co-accused, who had already committed a murder by the time the two of them met. Kitto, he said, had been easily dominated by Fontaine into doing what he wanted and had assisted Fontaine in trying to keep Mrs Scott-Elliot quiet only after Fontaine had knocked her to the floor first.

Yet, neither of them was convicted of actually murdering her. How did Fontaine manage that?

Obviously, the prosecution thought long and hard about the pleas eventually agreed, but had they been indicted on a single charge of murdering Mrs Scott-Elliot, how would Fontaine's story have withstood courtroom scrutiny?

Written years later, and in the certain knowledge of there being no further recriminations, Fontaine's contention that Kitto had become entranced by his expert knowledge of jewels and antiques which then led to Fontaine showing him round the flat, would surely have been attacked by both Kitto's counsel and the prosecution.

What 'expert' knowledge of jewels and antiques?

Apart from Fontaine's own pronouncements, there has never been any evidence of him having anything other than just about enough knowledge to realise that something might be worth the effort of stealing it. The 'guided tour' explanation, too, is absurd. In one version, Mrs Scott-Elliot was meant to be in a clinic and her sudden appearance at the bedroom door caught them off guard, but there is no mention of that in the other account in which Kitto pointlessly wandered behind Fontaine on his way to the wine cellar.

That Kitto reacted as Fontaine alleged seems strange; he was a small-time thief with no previous history of violence on his record, whereas Fontaine, as was pointed out, had already embarked on his murder career. But even if the court did not hear of Fontaine's previous violence nor his earlier convictions for possessing firearms, the method of suffocating her involved them acting together and would lead to a joint conviction if revealed.

The other scenario, with Kitto spontaneously deciding to clamp his hands round her face, sounds unlikely; like the rest of the persons Fontaine surrounded himself with, Kitto was an inadequate individual who was easily led. If there was any truth in Fontaine's assertion that Kitto spontaneously attacked the lady Fontaine was apparently so fond of, he ran the risk of Fontaine coming to her aid, particularly as the two men had just met and hardly knew each other.

And surely there would have been better ways to deal with the situation the two found themselves in. Could Fontaine – who was usually confident in his ability to charm ordinary mortals – not have made up an on-the-spot cover story about Kitto's presence there and thus smoothed things over?

Why was there blood to clear up if it happened in either of the ways Fontaine maintains? The plea in mitigation Mortimer gave to the court on Kitto's behalf appears a more likely account in that it must have come from Kitto alone, without Fontaine's influence, and involved Fontaine making the first aggressive move in knocking their victim to the floor before they finished her off.

The only feasible explanation for the murder of Dorothy Scott-Elliot was that Fontaine had already decided she should be the first of his two employers to die and that he would keep her husband alive long enough to facilitate the emptying of his bank accounts, depending on the old man's continued willingness to sign cheques. As long as he was kept sedated and malleable, they would also cruelly parade him round hotels and restaurants, in what must have been an attempt to keep up the pretence that both the Scott-Elliots were still alive.

The major flaw, of course, was that it was embarrassingly obvious that Mary Coggle would not have fooled anyone who knew the couple and a lurking suspicion remains that there had to be another, less obvious reason for the cruel masquerade. The time theoretically bought to allow them to clear artefacts from the Chelsea flat and drain bank accounts came at the cost of the bizarre party drawing unnecessary attention to themselves.

For that matter, why hire a car from the Scott-Elliots' flat rather than simply go to the hirer's premises, hire the car in a false name – which was done anyway – and avoid the possibility of a prosecution witness being able to identify all three of them? Was Fontaine simply enjoying the idea that the car-hire clerk would be impressed by his assumed identity and would think he was rubbing shoulders with the aristocracy?

The proposition that by moving the body to Scotland, they

stood themselves in better stead because of the existence of the 'Not Proven' verdict there, is noteworthy for its absurdity, not least because the murder would inevitably be traced back to London.

Whatever the rationale, they were by this point committed to their plan, and were now faced with the question of what to do with Walter Scott-Elliot – or 'The Captain' as he was known to friends, due to his rank and service in the Coldstream Guards in the Great War. The future did not look good for the elderly gentleman. There is little doubt that his wife, rather than falling victim to an unfortunate accident which necessitated an on-the-spot strategy, was simply assassinated in cold blood. Having thus far had his infirmity pitilessly exploited, seemingly to more easily siphon off his wealth, Mr Scott-Elliot did not have much time left to live.

33

HOSTAGE TO A PSYCHOPATH – THE MURDER OF WALTER TRAVERS SCOTT-ELLIOT

ARE WE CALLING HERE?

It was a truly nightmarish state of affairs.

The elderly gentleman was driven hundreds of miles in the company of a cold-blooded killer and his followers. They kept him drugged just short of unconsciousness, his dead wife was in the boot of the car and his own life was soon to end violently.

Walter Travers Scott-Elliot had been born on his family's Arkleton Estate near Langholm in the Scottish Borders in 1895. It had been in the family for generations, so Scott-Elliot had sold the estate with mixed feelings after he and his wife decided to base themselves in Chelsea. He had been educated at Eton before his service in the Great War, his post-war forwarding address being care of The Bombay Company, Box 109, Madras, India, which was the family business. The Scott-Elliots had a tradition of military service and commerce in the sub-continent and 'The Captain' spent his time there running the business and searching out and buying Indian antiques.

Ever the Edwardian gentleman, his first marriage in 1939 was to an Austrian Baroness Maria Alice von Groeller, who worked at the German Embassy in London. The wedding went ahead despite Joachim von Ribbentrop – Hitler's ambassador no less – personally warning her that if she went through with it, not only would there be reprisals against her family but she would be brought back to Austria 'one way or the other'.

133

Walter Scott-Elliot and his Baroness were not the sort of people who would be bullied, even if sinister reprisals were likely, and he whisked her off to the family estate at Arkleton to ensure her safety. Sad to say, the marriage did not survive the extraneous tensions and they divorced in 1948, although it is worth noting that the relationship outlived von Ribbentrop himself who was hanged following the Nuremberg Trials in 1946.

Scott-Elliot's second marriage in 1948 to Dorothy Nunn lasted until their murders nearly thirty years later. They existed in a refined atmosphere of wealth, appreciation of fine art and occasional continental trips to their houses in France and Italy.

Scott-Elliot was independent and unconventional. He had been described in some quarters as a Theosophist, a member of a nineteenth-century philosophical movement based on a belief that all world religions had something to offer human understanding, and it sought to provide an all-inclusive international system of religious tolerance and belief. Amongst other symbols, the Theosophical Society's seal incorporated both the Star of David and the Swastika, the latter being an ancient religious symbol long before it was permanently tarnished by the Nazis. Whilst there is little verifiable evidence of his involvement, it's not difficult to imagine the young Scott-Elliot embarking for India, fresh from France and Flanders, pondering human folly and finding comfort in such an all-inclusive and contemplative philosophy.

There is evidence, however, of Scott-Elliot's intellectual independence in his decision to join the Labour Party in 1937 – a most unusual move for a member of the land-owning aristocracy – and he became MP for Accrington in Lancashire for five years from 1945. He resigned from Parliament in 1950 to concentrate on his many directorships of various companies and his passion for collecting fine art. By that time, however, it's said that he had been shunned by the 'Borders Aristocracy' for treasonously becoming 'the laird of the left', one of the allegations against him being that he was in the habit of 'dining with his servants'.

In short, he was the sort of affluent, knowledgeable, compassionate and cultured human being that Fontaine deeply resented yet ached to become.

As they drove north, there were occasional signs that the old man was not as helpless as his captors hoped he would be. Left alone with Mary Coggle at the cottage at Newton Arlosh, he had insisted on taking his daily walk and she had been powerless to stop him. What a pity then that the local residents who later came forward to say they had noticed the confused and tired old gent didn't manage to intervene as he finished his constitutional and unwittingly made his way back into captivity.

Fontaine protracted the pleasure of controlling his 'master' to a merciless level, keeping him alive for six days for no obvious utilitarian purpose. The old man was incapable of doing anything that could have conceivably been of use to his captors, apart from signing cheques and paying bills, which in the grand scheme of things was small beer. Indeed, one of the mysteries in Fontaine's explanation, assuming the murder of Mrs Scott-Elliot was no mistake, is why he needed to kill either of his employers. He must have been aware that they were intending to visit relatives in Scotland a few days after she was killed, so why not wait until they were gone from the Chelsea flat then clear out as many valuables as he could before completing his stated intention of flying off to South America? Clearly enjoying the prolonged authority of deciding when Scott-Elliot was to die, Fontaine traipsed him about from hotel to restaurant to pub until his whim was satisfied.

Just before they killed him, they even decided to stop at the Struy Inn near Beauly in Inverness-shire for a drink, leaving their victim sleeping in the car. Ever keen to be seen in a good light – and even if it was just before the brutal murder of a defenceless old man – Fontaine bought tickets for a raffle for a local children's hospital as well as doubles for the trio. They panicked, however, when a local came in and informed them that the old man in the car asked that they hurry up as he wanted to go home. Again, it would have been potentially life-saving if some sign of the danger he was in could have communicated itself to members of the public, but the miserable truth is that Walter Scott-Elliot clearly had no idea he was about to die at their hands.

Even so, popping into an inn in a fairly remote area and drawing attention to yourself is explicable only if you believe you are either never going to face the consequences of the cowardly crime to come, or the temporary need to be flamboyant is more important at the time.

Perhaps the most poignant moment – for normal individuals – came when the four were driving north with Mrs Scott-Elliot's body in the boot and were in the vicinity of Kirtleton Estate. Recognising the area, which by sheer chance is only ten miles from the former Scott-Elliot family home at Arkleton near Langholm, Scott-Elliot suddenly became animated and excitedly asked his captors, like a child, if they were going to call in to his old house. When he was abruptly informed they were not, he hid his disappointment and talked at length about his childhood memories of happy days playing in the house and the gardens. As he talked the others kept a stony silence and eventually 'The Captain's' voice faded as he drifted off to sleep.

He would never see the Arkleton Estate again, as Fontaine had already decided that he had to die. Fontaine reasoned they couldn't release him as relatives would rapidly become suspicious, and in any event if their captive was not kept in a drugged state, he would soon realise what was going on.

In his account of the murder, Fontaine was at pains to share the blame amongst all of his cohorts, specifically stating that it was a joint decision to kill Scott-Elliot and they all had blood on their hands, but it's worth remembering that he had written, 'I couldn't trust the old man to stay doddery and confused if I let him go,' which obviously reflected the reality of the situation.

Their route north took them to a hotel in Blair Atholl in Perthshire where they stayed overnight, and then onto Inverness-shire where the murder took place. Fontaine alleged that Scott-Elliot had been killed after he had conveniently requested they stop the car so he could relieve himself. Fontaine helped him out of the car, then followed him and attempted to strangle him before Kitto finished the deed by fracturing his skull with a spade as Fontaine stood on his neck.

Again, there are variations in accounts. *The Prison Cell Confessions of Archibald Thompson Hall* tells of their shock when they realised their captive was awake in the car outside the pub in which they drank several large gins. Fontaine went into a foul mood and told Kitto to drive to a remote spot and when the car stopped, he forced Scott-Eliot to sign the remaining cheques. Scott-Elliot signed three then refused to do any more, angering Fontaine further. He dragged him out of the car, tore off his coat and threw it on the seat, and then pushed him to a fence and pushed him over. Kitto joined in and helped drag him towards a hedge where Fontaine knelt down beside the prostrate old man and pulled the woollen scarf he was wearing tightly round his neck, causing him to gag and choke. Suddenly Scott-Elliot seized Fontaine's wrists with an iron grip causing him to think that he was 'calling on the strength of his ancestors'. Realising that he would be unable to strangle him using just the scarf, Fontaine called on Kitto to help. Kitto then placed his hands round Scott-Elliot's neck and tried to strangle him as Fontaine kicked him in the chest.

Convinced the deed was done, the pair started to walk away but then heard a distinct groan, causing Fontaine to run back to the car to get the spade, which he gave to Kitto and told him to use it. Kitto brought it full force on the old man's head and it was finally over.

A LIVING TROPHY

A slightly different story from either of these, however, emerged after Fontaine's arrest. He insisted on writing out a statement, which included a description of the murder of Walter Scott-

Elliot. Apart from the unorthodox handwriting, he signed it 'Roy Hall' but initialled it 'RF' for 'Roy Fontaine' where corrections or additions were made. Having described taking lunch with 'Mr Scott' at a hotel near 'Abbington' and sticking strictly to his self-imposed code of not implicating any other – live – person, he continued in his own faltering style:

> I then moved with Mr Elliot North and stayed at Blair Atholl – I belive (TILT Hotel) where Mr Elliot payed By Cheque. Mrs Coggle travelled with me. We then travelled to Inverness where we visited a few Inns. Mr Scott Elliot Drinking whisky and a sandwich. We then drove towarDs a Place called muir. I recall a very small isolated PuB where the landLorD Spoke to Mr Scott, about a walking stick, within a short distance Mr Scott was Strangled with a woolen scarf. Mrs Coggle sat in car while this HaPPened, Mr Scott Being Stronger than I Had exPected. Near a River in forestry Commission Land. I left his Body Cover with Bushes. I am PrePared to assist Police to Locate Body.

In the margin of the page, and apparently to illustrate the burial site of the body, he drew a few lines and added 'Sketch of same (POOR) R F'. No reference to Kitto appears and the statement is remarkable for mentioning his victim in apparent conversation with a landlord about a walking stick, and – without any further lead-in – goes directly to him being strangled, as if both events were of equal significance.

Usually when a newspaper reports what 'friends' in prison have been told by someone recently convicted of a sensational series of murders, it has to be seen in the context of editorial pressure, but the report in the *Daily Express* for 2 November 1978 headed 'How I did it – by the butler' certainly has the hallmark of Fontaine bragging behind the scenes in prison. The article was written at the time of his appearance at the Old Bailey and mentions most of the features and phrases of the story Fontaine was later to try to convince biographers he was giving them exclusive access to, such as Scott-Elliot drawing strength from every ancestor he had in Scotland to try to stay alive. At least the article had the dubious advantage of being the first of many versions of the murders Fontaine was to peddle to 'friends', relations and journalists over the remaining years of his life.

In yet another account, he has Kitto getting the shovel to finish the old man off, following which he heard 'loud noises and realised that Mick had bludgeoned him to death'.

Whatever the true nature of Kitto's role, when he and Fontaine appeared at Edinburgh High Court in May 1978, both of them pleaded guilty to the murder of Walter Travers Scott-Elliot. The court heard that the pair had actually been spotted by a local girl as they returned from the murder scene, and she had described them as 'a pair of evil looking creatures'. Kitto had told the police that they had finally decided the old man 'had to go' and they 'found a clump of bushes, got the old man out of the car and killed him'.

The murder charge narrated that they had inflicted injuries on him 'from which he died and they did murder him' but the autopsy report, despite discovering a fractured mandible, was unable to determine a cause of death, due to the actions of predators destroying the tissues of the face, neck and chest.

A Lloyd's Bank chequebook was found in the right jacket pocket – presumably retained by Scott-Elliot in a final defiant act after he had flatly refused to sign more than three blank cheques. Whether he was aware of what they were about to do to him or not, it does seem that he was planning to urinate when he was attacked, with both his outer trousers, and the pyjama trousers he was found to be wearing underneath, being unbuttoned.

In court, attempting nonchalance, Fontaine reportedly smirked and said, 'Life begins at forty,' to the press benches as he was being taken away to start a life sentence, with a minimum of fifteen years; given that he was fifty-three at the time, it's perhaps not the best example of court room 'gallows humour' ever heard. Other reports attribute the remark to Kitto, which would at least be more accurate in terms of age, but it would have been more in the nature of their relationship if Fontaine *had* said it but on Kitto's behalf.

For his third murder, Fontaine's motives grow harder to decipher. Once again, it is difficult to see what advantage there was in Fontaine's plan to move the confused old man from place to place before dispatching him with the spade. It is notable, however, for being the first murder in which Fontaine willingly accepts partial blame, with no excuses of retribution or faulting the stupidity of others. Perhaps, considering the most lenient scenario, carting Scott-Elliot around was simply a stalling tactic as Fontaine tried to determine if they really had to kill the old man. Or, at the opposite extreme, he was simply another trophy to be flaunted whilst useful.

34

MURDERING MARY

SHE HAD A HEART OF GOLD DID MARY

Mary Coggle – known as 'Belfast Mary' – was, like the rest of the people Fontaine liked to surround himself with, criminally inclined but of the minor, 'nuisance value' variety. Fontaine had first met Mary at Whittingham Hospital in 1972 and had kept in touch with her so he could buy stolen documents such as chequebooks and driving licences from her.

Her role in the murder of the Scott-Elliots appears peripheral, certainly in terms of the actual physical attacks on them. She was said, however, to have been a housekeeper for the couple before Fontaine became an employee there. This fact, if true, gives her involvement a more ominous edge, as there then would be a strong suspicion that she passed on information about the tempting combination of conspicuous affluence and obvious vulnerability to Fontaine. Whilst there is reason to doubt that she ever worked at Richmond Court, of the five persons who could verify the fact, three were murdered by the other two.

According to Fontaine, after obtaining the job as the Scott-Elliots' new butler, he became aware of the tempting property near to their Richmond Court flat and Mary proposed Kitto as being agile enough to carry out Fontaine's plan to break in. She then made the introduction between the two who were soon to murder her.

After Mrs Scott-Elliot's murder, Fontaine told of taking Mary round various banks with her dressed as the deceased woman and successfully impersonating her, so that they could make large cash withdrawals. Fontaine also claimed, in *A Perfect Gentleman*, that Wootton came to London the day after the murder and the whole party travelled north with Mrs Scott-Elliot's body in the boot of Wootton's car. He seems to have forgotten that they did in fact hire a car from Godfrey Davis Car Hire in London, so any suggestion of Wootton's assistance at that early stage has to be doubted.

Whatever happened, Mary appears to have played the 'rich man's wife' to the best of her limited abilities and sometimes with excruciating results. As the 'master plan' – which seems too grand a title for their shambolic activities – belonged to Fontaine, he must have considered her capable of playing the allotted role that would net them a fortune. At the same time, there seems to have been a concurrent fantasy going on in Fontaine's cunning but restricted mind about him being able to exercise control over her as she acted the 'Lady'.

Prior to dumping Mrs Scott-Elliot's body in Comrie, Perthshire, they stopped for lunch in Crieff where the bewigged Mary overcompensated by acting out a caricature woman of means, and she did the same the next day when the strange expedition stayed overnight in a hotel in Blair Atholl. During their lunch break at the hotel in Crieff, Fontaine came up with a mystifying ruse, which suggested he was thoroughly enjoying being the puppet master. Unbeknown to the others, he left the hotel and called reception from a public call box nearby and left a message for 'Lady Scott-Elliot'. When a member of the hotel staff later enquired at their table for her, Kitto pointed Mary out. Perhaps it was an attempt to cajole her into taking her temporary new role in life more seriously, but it also hints at an ongoing fantasy being played out solely for Fontaine's gratification.

Following the murder of Mr Scott-Elliot, during which Mary sat in the car, the three of them drove to the Highland resort of Aviemore where the carefree Mary genuinely appears to have enjoyed herself. Ominously, of course, Fontaine noted that she had called friends in London to tell them of the 'high life' she was living. He warned her off making any more calls to friends, but when he and Kitto went to clear out the Scott-Elliots' flat, they left her in Newton Arlosh wherein, according to Fontaine, she risked their exposure to the authorities by 'swanning around' in the mink coat and jewels belonging to Mrs Scott-Elliot.

Indeed, one of the more puzzling aspects of her own slaying was her complete lack of insight into just how dangerous her situation was after the Scott-Elliots were murdered. One possible explanation is that she felt comfortable since she thought she was 'part of the team'. However, that she roused Fontaine's temper with her provocative and attention-seeking behaviour would not strike many as a good idea.

Fontaine and Kitto decided to reason with her, but if she proved awkward, Kitto promised to kill her after a final sex session. Accordingly, Fontaine tried the 'reasonable' approach with her; after all, the fur coat she had become deeply attached to had Dorothy Scott-Elliot's initials sewn into the lining. He promised her that if she saw sense and agreed to get rid of it, he would buy her another one. Mary appeared to see the logic of what had been explained to her, so he was able to let Kitto know that he was free to have his way with her without having to kill her afterwards. Fontaine then recorded a second trip to London for more of the murdered couple's precious items, but then recalled his dismay on his return as she had again been 'parading around' the village, thus sealing her fate.

After he and Kitto had killed her, they dumped her in a stream near Middlebie in Dumfriesshire at mid-morning on 18 December 1977. They then drove to London, lived in the Scott-Elliot flat for a while, sold antiques during the day, and ate in the best restaurants and took in West End shows in the evenings.

PLAYING WITH FIRE

Fontaine's earlier account of what led up to the murder was different. He recalled the trio going to an Edinburgh hotel, with

Fontaine calling himself Walter Scott-Elliot so he could use up one of the cheques he had forced the frail old man to sign just before his murder. As a joke – which Mary didn't notice – he booked her in as 'Mrs Block of Hudson Street, London', 'Hudson' being both the name of a television butler at the time and, of course, the name of the former employer he bore the developing grudge against; 'Block' presumably was a comment on her intelligence. As he checked out of the hotel the next day, he noticed calls to London in the bill – paid for with the Scott-Elliot cheque – and it began to annoy him. He quizzed her about the calls and she assured him that she had said nothing about where she was and had only called to let friends know she was alright.

Whilst in Edinburgh, he ordered Mary to sell off some stolen antiques, which she did, but she appears to have been soundly diddled by the city's antique dealers; Fontaine reasoned that at least the stolen items were being widely distributed round the country.

Matters seemed to be settled and they stopped for a drink before going back to the cottage. Mary slept with Kitto that night and the next morning, she cooked them breakfast, after which all three went to the local pub and drank until mid-afternoon. They chatted with and bought drinks for the locals and in the evening they dressed and went out for dinner at a nearby hotel.

In the course of their meal, Mary suddenly announced she was leaving for London the next day. They tried to dissuade her but she wouldn't budge, so at the cottage they explained that if she were to go, she would have to leave the mink coat as it would easily be traced back to them. Fontaine then said that they would drive her to the station immediately if she packed her bags, but as she left the room to gather her clothes together, he picked up a poker and placed it on the mantelpiece. Neither man said a thing but both knew what was about to happen.

On her return from the bedroom, and as they faced each other, he said, 'Well it looks like goodbye, Mary,' before he struck her with the poker. He had aimed at her head but caught her shoulder and she fell to the floor. Kitto pounced on her and tied her hands behind her back. As Fontaine raised the poker a second time, she pleaded for her life saying he could trust her, but he went ahead and smashed her skull in.

As Fontaine stripped the body, Kitto poured them a drink and they re-dressed her in male apparel. They then removed her wig and placed a plastic bag over her head before stuffing the body under a bed until they disposed of it the next day.

The next evening they carried her out to the car and put her in the boot before driving north. Kitto, who always drove, had requested that they didn't travel too far this time and they ended up at Middlebie where they stopped at the bridge over the Black Burn and tumbled the body from the plastic sheeting they had wrapped it in, twenty feet into the water below, then drove off as quickly as they could.

Mary's body must have lain beneath the bridge before it drifted into view and was seen from the road above on Christmas Day 1977. A seventeen-year-old farm worker, who was making his way home for Christmas dinner, spotted the body from his elevated position in a tractor cab. The site chosen to dispose of the body and the trouble taken to dress it in male clothes points to an expectation on Fontaine's part of it being easily discovered, although the police were apparently to be fooled into investigating the case as a 'lesbian murder'.

After that, the hope was that she could not be traced, even though she clearly had been in bother with the police before and would be on file. To that end, Fontaine made a call himself to one of her regular London haunts and told one of her friends that she had met a wealthy man and that they got on so well that imminent wedding bells wouldn't surprise him.

That, together with the 'lesbian murder' ploy, seems to be the extent of thought Fontaine put into avoiding detection. Mary's friends knew who she was meant to be with and, standing an unusual outbreak of murderous activity in lesbian circles, the post-murder strategy looks pretty feeble.

And to add to the bizarre picture, Fontaine came up with yet another account of her last moments in the self-written statement he gave after he had been arrested. In that one, he said the pair of them had been arguing over the coat and that he had stopped the car at the bridge to urinate. She then, apparently, came over to stand beside him, and when he asked her to look over the bridge, he shoved her over the edge. A half-hearted attempt was also made to explain her attire, saying he had 'broken' his tie on a tree, so he put it round her arm. Overall, however, it's a puzzle why he thought the written statement was worth the effort.

The location of the bridge is on a bend in the road and although traffic is light, approaching vehicles cannot easily be seen or heard, so Fontaine's earlier account of quickly discarding the body before speeding away sounds far more likely. Anyone going to the bother of scrambling down the embankment to place the body in the burn not only runs the risk of detection by reason of unexplained and eccentric behaviour, but also has to demonstrate an agility, which, of the two, only Kitto would have had. Finally, any car parked at or near the bridge for even a short time would be quickly noticed, not least because it would cause something of a minor road block, so it all points to a hasty disposal of the body.

SHE HAD IT COMING

When it comes to the details of how Mary was killed, Fontaine's account checks out. The post mortem report showed lacerations to the head and large bruises to the left ear, left shoulder and left arm, the cause of death being the blow to the head, which caused a massive haemorrhage to the base of the brain, undoubtedly caused by Fontaine's blow with the poker.

Yet, when it comes to a confirmation of *why* Mary was killed, none is available. He claimed that Mary was being stubborn about giving up the coat and compromising their situation with her wanton behaviour, but surely using those actions as justification for killing a woman whom he professed fondness for is absurd, even by Fontaine's standards.

Despite the alleged spontaneity of the decision to kill Mary, evidence seems to prove otherwise. By the time it came to transporting Mary's corpse, an activity which Fontaine and Kitto were becoming quite adept at, there was a ready availability of a presumably large quantity of plastic sheeting for wrapping up bodies – which does have an untypical element of organisation about it.

And even if Mary did become attached to the notion of keeping the mink – it would perhaps have been difficult for her not to in those days of guilt-free fur wearing – why her suspected overall untrustworthiness was not predicted by either of her accomplices is a mystery. There are two possible explanations. It is likely, if he really knew her as well as he claimed, that Fontaine was aware of Mary's unreliable nature and had planned to get rid of her after she was no longer useful to him anyway. The other option is that he was simply unable to see beyond the Scott-Elliots' riches until the murders were safely out of the way and only then did he realise the risk Mary posed.

The former seems to be implied by his personally superior view of his fourth victim as reported by the *News of the World*:

> She was a crooked woman and I was a crooked fellow and we were of use to each other. But she wasn't the kind of woman I admire. She was rough and coarse and had the most atrocious accent. In a way, that led to her death.

Even if it is probable that Fontaine was planning to kill Mary all along, exactly what her role was in the whole Scott-Elliot proceedings remains unclear, aside from unconvincingly masquerading as Mrs Scott-Elliot. How that assisted any financial ingathering of the old couple's wealth is not easy to see, except for suggesting that Mrs Scott-Elliot was still alive, albeit in a new, downmarket guise, which theoretically allowed them more time in which to carry out their plan.

Once again, the temptation is to assume that Mary's role-playing principally served to titillate Fontaine's disproportionate obsession with wealth and aristocracy, with him in an all-important controlling position. This conjecture is underlined in Fontaine's final account of the murder of Mary Coggle, even though it comes on the back of the encouragement he obviously extracted from press coverage of his criminal activities down the years, and is most likely just another example of him spicing up a story for salacious public consumption. In this later story, not only was Kitto going to have sex with Mary one final time before murdering her, but she also appears in the offending mink and demands sex with Fontaine, a detail missing from his earlier account of events. The depiction of Mary's prostration before him underlines his need to be seen as sexually powerful.

He was obsessed with being in control, and it is likely that casting Mary as a Lady held a particular role-reversal pleasure for him. If that was the case, Mary's murder was either inevitable from the beginning, as Fontaine revelled in holding the ultimate authority of deciding when she should die, or else he made the decision after he simply tired of the charade.

Once again, and as with Mrs Scott-Elliot's murder, Fontaine expressed regret about 'having to kill a friend' but even if he could unconvincingly attempt to explain why Mrs Scott-Elliot's murder was 'necessary', he fell short in Mary's case for the simple reason that it was never clear why she had to be involved at all; her only crucial act was in introducing Fontaine to Kitto. Sadly, it was that very first involvement that could have, in fact, been her downfall. If Fontaine killed her for knowing too much, her offence went back to the very introduction of him and Kitto to each other and thenceforth being conscious of what they were up to. His regret is as sincere as his arithmetic is good – she had been a 'friend', he said, for nearly ten years, yet he killed her six years after they met for the first time.

Certainly, if Fontaine killed Mary for knowing too much, that also obviously applied to Kitto and would thus have had serious implications for his continued wellbeing had the pair not been apprehended when they were. In fact, the *News of the World* for 5 November 1978 not only reported that Fontaine had vowed to kill Kitto for 'grassing' on him after they had been arrested, but it also claimed Fontaine had said, 'I'd planned to kill him anyway after the other murders. I thought that if he was out of the way, there wouldn't be trouble from anyone.'

The paper also reported a pact between Kitto and Fontaine based on mutual distrust, whereby if one of them had a gun, the other would keep the cartridges or vice versa. That, though, has the stamp of Fontaine's Hollywood fixation about it.

One thing was certain by that time – Fontaine had reached the point of no return. He was now comfortable with murder and willing to commit such a crime to fulfill his own needs and desires. Kitto was, without a doubt, next on Fontaine's list of those who 'needed to go'. However, a phone call from Wootton would, temporarily at least, mean that the murder of Kitto in Fontaine's unpredictable priorities was to be displaced by that of another less fortunate soul – Fontaine's brother, Donald.

35

THE MURDER OF
DONALD MCMILLAN THOMSON HALL

UNFINISHED BUSINESS

On 15 October 1977, two young girls from Edinburgh went for a night out on the city's Royal Mile. They were last seen alive with two men in a pub called The World's End and when their bodies were found the next day, ten miles away on the coast in East Lothian, a double murder enquiry began. Thirty years later, with the advent and development of DNA, Angus Robertson Sinclair stood trial for and was acquitted of the murders, following a successful legal submission by his counsel regarding the sufficiency of evidence against him.

At the time of the killings, though, the intensive police investigation followed up all possible leads to no avail, and members of the public were urged to contact the police should they notice anything suspicious that might be linked to the outrageous double rape and murder.

The town of North Berwick lies outside Edinburgh on the same coastline the murder victims' bodies were found on, and shopkeepers, garage attendants and landladies were all asked to report anything that might assist in solving the terrible crimes.

Three months later, on the evening of Monday 16 January 1978, Fontaine and Kitto checked into the Blenheim House Hotel in the town and Mr Wight, the proprietor, sensed something about the pair that niggled him. On the alert anyway after the recent murders, Wight's antenna was finely tuned. Fontaine's glibness, which sometimes worked so well, was a non-starter with the suspicious hotelier, and the more the dubious guest talked, the deeper Wight's doubts became about the dapper man with the red and white spotted hanky flamboyantly overhanging his breast pocket.

Fontaine's practised ability to deceive others must have wavered, and it seemed to Wight that he appeared anxious about completing the necessary registration particulars. He and Kitto were, of course, using false names. Fontaine chattered on about touring Scotland before the pair emigrated to Australia and as soon as he completed the paperwork, they went straight into the bar and started downing double brandies.

As they wined and dined, Wight's suspicions were corroborated by his wife; she said they made her feel uneasy. Wight was now inclined to suspect, at the very least, that a board and lodgings fraud was being enacted, so he called the police. Even after they arrived, Fontaine and Kitto might easily have extricated themselves from suspicion by 'confirming' their identities, or even by paying the bill in advance.

Providence, however, intervened.

They had changed the registration plates on their hired Ford Granada, principally to avoid paying the hire company, but something made Fontaine feel queasy about the car's original registration number as well. VGE 999 R looked and sounded ominous for the career criminal – and so it proved to be, but *not* because it looked like the emergency services number. When the replacement plate was checked on the national computer it actually referred to an entirely different model of car, a Ford Escort owned by the company Mothercare.

Little wonder, then, that Fontaine was having trouble keeping up his usually slick façade; the murderous pair were, of course, travelling in what was in effect a stolen car, the number plates failed to match up with the tax disc and, as the police were soon to discover, the body of Donald McMillan Thomson Hall was in the boot.

And there they were, enjoying brandies and the after-glow of murder when the police appeared and casually enquired about the discrepancy between plate and disc. Keeping as calm as they could, they answered the police questions, Fontaine maintaining that they had a loan of the car from a John Harvey, his sister Violet's husband's name. Eventually the police obliged them to go to North Berwick police office to clear matters up. Fontaine was allowed to go to the bathroom not once but twice – after all it was a minor investigation and could easily have been resolved – where he took advantage of the relative permissiveness by destroying bogus documents in his possession before, on the second occasion, climbing out of the bathroom window and escaping.

The Metropolitan Police had been making enquiries too. Antiques known to belong to the Scott-Elliots had been turning up in shops around the country, including valuable Meissen china recovered in Newcastle-under-Lyme, and the Scott-Elliots themselves had disappeared. Relatives in Inverurie, Aberdeenshire, had expected to see them, as Mrs Scott-Elliot had booked flights to Aberdeen in December in order to pay them a visit, but the couple had simply not shown up. Mrs Scott-Elliot's niece, who had a dinner engagement with her, also found it strange when she phoned the flat at Richmond Court to try to find out why her aunt had not shown up and Fontaine, who had been clearing the flat of works of art, had the arrogance and ill-judgement to answer the call. His explanation that Mrs Scott-Elliot had gone on holiday and that the niece must have the wrong date caused puzzlement. The caretaker at the flat had thought the couple might be abroad but he reported having seen their butler and another man visiting the flat recently.

Whatever Fontaine considered himself adept at, it wasn't thinking ahead. Even without Mr Wight's intuition, the net had been closing in on the slipshod pair; when police went to the Scott-Elliots' flat they found it ransacked and there were bloodstains on the carpets and the doorstep.

It's all the more mystifying, then, that they were caught in the mundane way they were.

WHAT TO DO WITH DONALD?

In 1999, Fontaine described Donald as his half-brother and, unlike his obsessively well-groomed self, he said Donald was dirty, unkempt and had paedophilic traits. Donald had been released from Haverigg Prison in Cumbria on 13 January 1978, having served three years for housebreaking. He had gone from the prison to the house his step-father John Wootton had shared with Marion in Lytham, before her death from cancer in 1975. According to Fontaine, Wootton then called him asking for his advice, as it seemed Donald intended to stay there.

Fontaine was against the idea, but not out of concern for his step-father's welfare. He reasoned that Donald would jeopardise Wootton's usefulness to him. In the past, Wootton had always been available to help Fontaine in his many scrapes and had proved willing to drop everything to drive hundreds of miles when required. Fontaine needed him to stay in the shadows and Donald's small time thievery might attract police attention to Wootton's house.

The solution? Donald 'had to go'. According to that version, Wootton's only comment when Fontaine told him that he and Kitto would 'put Donald to rest' was that they should 'be careful'.

Fontaine, then, had made his mind up that Donald was to die, the only question being when the right opportunity would arise. The time came, incredibly, on the very first night Donald stayed at the cottage at Newton Arlosh, three days after his release back into society.

In a previous version, Fontaine said that when Donald was released from prison, at Fontaine's suggestion, he had gone to a pub in Preston where they were to meet. When his older brother failed to show up, Donald carried on drinking and became steadily more intoxicated, so by the time he made it to Wootton's house that night, he was in a sorry state.

153

Despite the arrangement he had suggested, that night Fontaine had instead gone out with Kitto, and John and Caroline Wootton for a meal, making it clear how little he thought of his brother. They later met up with Donald at the house and after discussing the problem about what should be done with him, it was decided that he should go with Fontaine and Kitto to Newton Arlosh the next day. They drove there the following day and that night went to several pubs in Carlisle with Donald again getting drunk.

By the time they got home, Donald was in no state to discuss their ongoing plans to rob Lady Hudson at Kirtleton House, but the next morning he was enthusiastic when the plan was explained to him, so they drove there in daylight to consider matters before returning home to the cottage that night. They decided that the plan was worth going ahead with, but reasoned they would need face masks to avoid recognition.

However, as they continued to discuss it, it suddenly occurred to Fontaine that letting Donald into the scheme at all was actually a big mistake; he would undoubtedly blab when drunk, as he often was. The dilemma he now had was that he had taken him into his confidence and couldn't undo that fact, nor ask him to simply forget what he had been privy to. His hatred of Donald also came to the fore when it suddenly hit him that if anything happened to either him or Wootton, Donald would have access to 'his daughter' Caroline and she would be in danger of molestation, given Donald's perverted propensities.

When the talk was of tying Lady Hudson and Mrs Lloyd up, Donald became animated and mentioned his technique for just such an occasion. After he went into the bedroom for a piece of pyjama cord, Fontaine and Kitto exchanged glances; they had 'another Mary' on their hands and their opportunity had arisen. Donald came back into the living room with the cord and got Kitto to tie him up. Fontaine quickly took advantage of this volunteered vulnerability to slap a chloroformed pad over Donald's nose and mouth, but had to pour the anaesthetic down his throat before he succumbed to its effects.

Fontaine then put a plastic bag over Donald's head and

stripped the body; on finding a photograph of their mother and young Caroline in his pocket, Fontaine became enraged and tore it into pieces. They then put the body into a filled bath.

BLOOD BROTHERS

Only Fontaine maintained that Donald and he were half-brothers. He claimed that Donald's real father was an army major Marion had an affair with in 1940, but other available evidence points to Donald genuinely being Archibald senior's son.

Archibald actually arranged for his wife to go into a private clinic during her confinement, no doubt an unusual step for the time. He also registered the birth and remembered Donald in his will.

There is of course a presumption of paternity in marriage anyway and it may be that Archibald decided simply to go along with things, but Fontaine's irrational hatred of Donald as being only a 'half-brother' looks very much like another mythical reason dragged in to try to validate past events; many half-brothers co-exist peacefully and the usual source of conflict is when families fall out and the children are forced to take sides. Fontaine's obsession with, and dislike of, Donald's allegedly different paternity might be more easily understood if, say, his parents had split up and he had taken his father Archibald's side in a bitter dispute over Marion's alleged infidelity, but it was almost the opposite. Fontaine considered Archibald to be a fool for being loyal, honest and hard-working whilst he extolled the increasingly unpredictable Marion's many 'virtues'.

Maybe the real reason for his antipathy towards Donald stemmed from as far back as 1940 when Fontaine's shrine to Hitler was discovered in the Catterick army base and the family was sent home in disgrace. The story about Marion's affair might have been concocted simply to upstage or cover up his own embarrassment over his subversive teenage activities, although that theory is based on the uncertain premise of Fontaine experiencing shame in any form.

Donald, however, being the younger brother and presumably taking attention away from Fontaine, earned himself the scorn and enduring hatred of his older brother, and considering Fontaine's mental instability, he was eager to add one more murder to the list not least because it meant snuffing out the existence of one whom he had always wished dead.

Fontaine had taken advantage of a fairly straightforward opportunity to get rid of Donald, but now he was in possession of yet another dead body that he and Kitto had to dispose of. The snow storm which caused them to head for North Berwick seems never to have happened, at least in the intensity described, and in yet another version, from 1978, he is alleged to have said that they had set off intending to go north but 'for some reason he was to regret', they made for the town.

Justifying and explaining the unjustifiable and the inexplicable can sometimes be difficult, particularly if the storyteller himself is unwilling to reveal the truth about what really motivated him. Donald's alleged improprieties towards young girls stemmed largely from the minor incident in a cinema when he was a teenager and which brought a police caution – no doubt an entirely different and far more robust 'warning', probably involving a boot to the backside, compared to the modern equivalent. Perhaps the one previously mentioned genuine reason for his hatred of Donald was that he might have informed the authorities about Fontaine's whereabouts which led to his arrest in Weston-super-Mare when he was on the run in 1966, and Fontaine simply kept the grudge warm until he could act on it.

Having 'another Mary' on their hands and justifying his murder on those grounds is absurd. Knowing both Mary and Donald well, there can be no excuse for failing to realise, until it was too late and they were privy to the plans, that they were the sort of people who would be unable to exercise discretion and, as such, would be future liabilities. As with Mary, it's not clear what role Donald was to play in Fontaine's illegal activities and the excuse advanced for his murder is unconvincing; both Mary and Donald were simply victims of Fontaine's indulgence – he did it because he could and was on a killing spree.

Perhaps what Fontaine later allegedly told a reporter was closest to the truth, given that his brother was his fifth victim: 'With Donald, I knew that one death more or less wasn't going to make very much difference.'

Once again, Fontaine clearly saw himself as superior to the general public and he demonstrated the typical mistaken belief of the psychopath that he could hoodwink the rest of the world. For a certain percentage of the population, that sort of arrogance actually triggers alarm bells and to this day, Mr Wight is unable to specify the exact reason for his suspicions. Indeed, Mr Wight clearly did not fall into the category of person Fontaine liked to manipulate, namely old, vulnerable or criminally flawed and something akin to realisation of that fact might account for his eventual unwillingness to take his chances with juries, the bulk of whom do not fall into that group.

Fontaine and Kitto would, of course, have been arrested for the thefts and murders sooner or later, but had the road tax disc been altered to coincide with the registration plates, they might have been able to leave the hotel the next morning, dump Donald's body somewhere on the coast, burn his hands to destroy his fingerprints, and continue their criminal ways.

That they were not, naturally, wasn't Fontaine's fault and he roundly blamed the 'stupid' Kitto for them being detected and convicted. However, within months of being arrested for the final time, he told a reporter from the *Daily Express*:

The car we were driving was one which we had hired from Godfrey Davis some months previous but latterly I had decided that there was no point in paying £150 per week rental and had obtained false number plates. We just chose the numbers at random and had them made up in a number plate factory.

What would have happened had they not been picked up at North Berwick? Did he really think that the police might not be interested in interviewing the Scott-Elliots' butler after the old couple had disappeared? If there was anything akin to a plan in Fontaine's head it was apparently to steal as much as he could then head for the mythical 'place in the sun' to while away his final days in what he regarded as well-earned luxury. Before that, there seems little doubt that Lady Hudson would have been subjected to an unwelcome nocturnal visit involving chloroform and rope, after which Kitto would then have had a limited lifespan.

Once Kitto was arrested he quickly caved in and told the police all about the killings, and when police searched their hotel room they found seventy-six silver Edward I pennies stolen from the flat at Richmond Court. As we have seen, however, Fontaine maintained the fiction of not mentioning any other person, in line with his self-professed 'no grassing' policy, which was part of his apparent 'don't do harm to your own kind' philosophy. It can be assumed therefore that exceptions – in the shape of Mary and Donald – *were* permitted and doing 'harm to your own' was allowed if circumstances changed. Fontaine's own personal exceptions extended from murder to stealing; the ever-loyal Wootton might not have noticed, but Fontaine had stolen a credit card from him and hidden it in an outhouse on Kirtleton Estate, causing him to have to retrieve it under cover of darkness one night after his dismissal.

At least one reason why Fontaine took to telling his story – and several versions of it – was to try to convince the rest of the world that he was really only following 'alternative' rules, conventional standards being patently unfair towards highly talented but socially victimised persons like himself. In truth, the only 'rules' Fontaine adhered to were the ones that suited him at any particular time, excluding consideration of anyone else.

No wonder Lady Hudson slept with a loaded firearm in her

bedroom even after Fontaine received his life sentence. After all, if it's true that four new serial killers emerge every year in America, there had to be other Fontaines out there in 1970s Britain.

36

THE OXYGEN OF PUBLICITY

Following his final arrest, and nearly forty years after the 'Hitler shrine' incident in Catterick, Fontaine made one more attempt at evading ultimate justice by copying the do-or-die mentality of top-ranking Nazis. He had professed admiration for their belief in ranking an honourable suicide above capture and punishment by the enemy.

So, imagining he was following the examples of Hitler, Goering and Goebbels, Fontaine elected for noble self-destruction. He wrote that he would rather die than spend the rest of his life in prison, so after his final arrest he swallowed the barbiturates he had hidden about his person.

Whilst a medical team worked to save Fontaine's life, Kitto revealed all, and by the time Fontaine was revived, the evidence was building to an inescapable conclusion. A police spokesman, with an admirable turn of phrase, said, 'This case covers the whole spectrum from high society to almost incomprehensible villainy.'

Opponents of capital punishment almost invariably base their disagreement with the practice on the notion that state retribution lowers all the citizens of that particular country to the level of the perpetrator and, in order for civilised behaviour to prevail, it's vital that the state follows a more enlightened path.

Its difficult to disagree, but the misery Fontaine claims to have experienced in serving a sentence of natural life also has to be considered. He 'campaigned' to be euthanised and made what appeared to be a genuine effort to die through a prolonged hunger strike. If execution or suicide is the easy way out of escaping a long reflective jail sentence, why do so many felons desperately plea bargain to save their skins in jurisdictions which do impose capital punishment? Do they have to settle into, then come to terms with the despair of their situation before the penny drops? Fontaine's request to be given 'a pill and a glass of wine' was made in a letter to *The Observer* in March 1995. At the time he was in Full Sutton maximum security prison near York, was the oldest prisoner serving a natural life sentence and was one of fourteen convicted murderers the Home Secretary had written to, telling them they would never be released. In his semi-literate style, he declared:

> You must be aware at trials Scotland and Old Bailey I plead guilty. No waste of time. Long trial at public expense. At 72 years of age I live a quite [sic] life. Daily praying for Death. Why not ask the government to give mercy killing a pill and a glass of wine. Would save the country so much waste of money. Yes.

Rather than concern for the public purse, his request should be seen in the context of the prison system he was forced to live in. He was said to be 'desperately unhappy' about having to mix with rapists, terrorists, drug dealers and – astonishingly – murderers. Indeed, he exhibited typical selfish psychopathic anxiety about the possibility of anything harmful happening to himself, and was terrified about the prospect of the reintroduction of capital punishment before his case was heard in the Old Bailey in 1978. He also seems to have developed a fixation with his own death from a terminal illness, but each time he was medically examined, the prison doctors found him remarkably fit and simply feeling sorry for himself.

Fontaine had used hunger striking as a tactic to try to force the prison authorities to do what he wanted several times, and in the first instance, he claimed he had succeeded. Having disappeared from a prison hostel and fled to Dublin in 1975, he was sent to Walton Prison in Liverpool. In the manner of an effete hotel guest, he found the place too dirty for his tastes and refused food for four weeks until he was granted a transfer back to Long Lartin Prison. Whether he was due to be relocated there or not, he was actually transferred and Fontaine saw it as a victory over the system and tried to use the tactic again at a later date.

The second time was in Hull Prison in July 1979 when he refused food – with the exception of the occasional pie or bar of chocolate – for a reported 352 days. What *can* be verified is that his weight shrank from thirteen to six stones.

The issue that prompted that strike was that he felt he should be sent to a prison amongst his 'ain folk' in Scotland. His blood count fell and he lapsed into unconsciousness, but he was steadfast in his aim. Extra visits were allowed in anticipation of his imminent death and he later claimed that his former wife Ruth came to see him and put fresh flowers round his room. An official from the Home Office came to see him and told him they were very sorry, but, 'the Home Office would not submit to blackmail. If I wished to die, then so be it. I could die here or live here. That was my choice. I fell back into unconsciousness.' It was a matter of principle and Fontaine was not the sort the prison authorities should meet head-on.

Or was he?

Without any attempt at explaining why the issue of a transfer suddenly became unimportant, he capitulated and took soup, once again claiming his 'will to survive was too strong'.

It was reported in the *Daily Mirror* for 27 May 1980 that Fontaine had in fact been taking Holy Communion three times a day during his protest, finding that the wine 'soothed' his pain; it also described how he asked which religion allowed wine to be given to the communicant before electing for the faith of his choice.

It looks like the Home Office official assessed the situation correctly and, together with the noticeable absence of public clamour for the prisoner to be returned to the land of his birth, the whole melodramatic charade was exposed as yet another cheap shot at self publicity. Indeed, it's also worth noting that after his life sentence was imposed at Edinburgh in May 1978, he was on record as saying he was looking forward to his transfer south so he could be moved to the 'more civilised' English prison system.

Fontaine also came up with the ruse that he had committed other, as yet undetected murders. He said this mainly to attract attention, but also with an eye on making money. This time he let it slip that there were two more bodies, one of them belonging to a helicopter pilot who had been recruited to help spring a prisoner from Parkhurst, but who had fallen out with the wrong people. In an attempt to validate the story, he had written a letter outlining the plan and made sure the police got hold of it. With his track record, the authorities were certainly obliged to check the story, but as no pilots were reported missing, the pretence was rapidly exposed as an attempt to gain attention and extract money from the press.

The letter itself is childishly obvious in its effort to spark off both a police enquiry and a press feeding frenzy. 'Robin' was Kitto's other name and the Mary he referred to was Mary Coggle.

Isle of Wight
28/11/77

Dear Robin,
Sorry I missed your phone call but Mary and I were out at another hotel. It's bloody cold here and I'll be glad to be back in London. There is no problem in renting a house here. We looked at a couple today. But over last night, I looked at Woolton Creek and the boat could be left there once it's repainted. I had to be careful as the Newport police know me down here, but Mary does well. She loves this kind of life.

The airport here is not a good proposition, not like ours at Newton Arlosh and the scream will go up so quickly, all planes will be checked.

I took a load of photos of all about Parkhurst and these glasses I have are good. I saw the Security Block easily, glad I'm not in it. I hope you have everything stocked up at the cottage. It's best we have a lot of tinned food there. I think this will be a harder place to pull out of than L Lartin. Once on the canal it should be no problem provided the other fellows can land there OK. But it's a big compound and I've all the measurements of it.

Keep up the front that I'm in London on business. These locals are a nosy lot. Once the Elliots go to Italy, Mary is ready to start on their bank accounts so that without any problem we have plenty of expense money. I looked at Cadbury's place. He has a copter but I like Ferrantis, very rich family.

Mary and I had a lovely dinner last night but I feel stupid with this bloody wig on. Mary says it looks OK. Maybe that's the Bacardi talking. I'll do my best to get up to the cottage next weekend but I've got to keep everything sweet at the flat. I'll have to stop wearing this watch, it's too easily noticed. A bit flash down here. I'll get you one for Christmas. Do you think we should go back up to Aberdeen again? I don't want our friend getting a change of heart but I doubt it as he is greedy for money. Anyway, with these guns he will do as he is told. I'll visit the Lancelot as arranged and meet you there with Mary. I'm going to take Mrs Scott there to see how the other half live. She'll enjoy it. VIP treatment.

So Mary sends love, and behave yourself.

Best regards,

Roy

No sailing for me, the water looks bloody rough and cold.

It was embarrassingly clear the letter was bogus, but, after recent events, the police had to follow it up. Violet had handed it over to them after its 'discovery' and Fontaine was interviewed about its contents. He must have been ecstatic.

The *Daily Express* for 7 November 1979 also reported that in a 'death bed confession' Fontaine had told his ex-wife Ruth that there were *four* other murders he wanted to clear up, obliging the police to dig up some of Lady Hudson's ground at Kirtleton looking for a murdered American helicopter pilot called Reynolds. Fontaine said Reynolds had been tested to see if he could be trusted before being asked to take part in the springing of prisoners form Parkhurst, but had failed the test and was suffocated using a plastic bag and a tie.

In truth, Fontaine could have survived more easily without food than without media attention. Aside from his publicised 'plea' for state euthanasia in 1995, Fontaine's opportunities for press-engendered notoriety dwindled, and he had to content himself with petty 'victories' over prison staff, complaints about the violence and lack of respect shown by younger prisoners towards him, and grumbling about the utter indignity of being one of the few 'natural lifers' left in the prison system. Despite – or possibly because of – all his years in prison, he was in decent physical shape and survived for twenty-four years in his final spell of self-pitying captivity.

He died of a series of strokes at Queen Alexandra Hospital, Portsmouth, having been transferred there from Kingston Prison, on 16 September 2002 aged seventy-eight, the Death Certificate wrongly recording an 'alias' date of birth Fontaine sometimes used, 17 June instead of 17 July 1924. By then he was the oldest 'natural lifer' in the system.

After his death, Archibald Thomson Hall, aka Roy Fontaine, left behind vastly exaggerated and contradictory accounts of his bizarre criminal life. As we have seen, little of what he said can be verified, leaving the motivation behind many of his actions undeterminable, so the question has to be asked – what drove him on his own peculiar route through life?

PART III:

THE MAKING OF A MONSTER

37

WAS HE STAR-STRUCK?

It has to be conceded that any attempt to understand or explain the deeds of someone with Fontaine's personality disorder by studying the outside influences in his life is ultimately destined to fail. Who can really say what motivates another person, particularly when they repeatedly face punishment for making the same mistakes?

Despite that, the trail has a promising starting point that is fairly easy to follow; as the psychopath acts almost exclusively in his own interests, it seems virtually inevitable that someone or something at an early stage of his development caused him to think that such a selfish lifestyle was acceptable and understandable to others. Presumably he is either reinforced in that belief by the actions or inactions of those around him or he somehow imagines that to be the case, and so goes on to walk a tightrope of self-delusion.

Perhaps the first clue to Fontaine's dangerous mindset can be seen in the influence of Hollywood.

MOVIE MADNESS

The impact of new forms of media can often be overlooked and taken for granted as time goes by. Today's younger generation have a talent for technology that sometimes unsettles their parents and mystifies their grandparents. The increasing importance of computers, mobile phones and the Internet in everyday life has led to a situation where their absence would be catastrophic to many.

But it's all happened before.

The glittering celluloid world of the movies had a massive effect on society during the inter-war years and offered a temporary refuge from the grind of everyday life during the Great Depression and the Second World War. In fact, during the war years, the movies were a compulsive distraction that sent out messages of hope and certainty for better times ahead. Sir Beverley Baxter, who had the privilege of being an MP for nearly thirty years from 1935 on, and the dubious privilege of allegedly attending a party Fontaine claimed to have been at, wrote:

> In parts of Lancashire where life is very grim and one sees the local cinema palace and its perhaps slight vulgarity, but there it is, a magic door at which people can leave the hardships of reality, and, for two or three hours, be carried away on wings of song or phantasy.

Once radio and cinema got into their stride, previous forms of entertainment such as live theatre were eventually eclipsed and the sheer novelty of radio broadcasting and the emergence of local cinemas made a huge impact. It's estimated that by as early as 1930, weekly audiences in America amounted to an astonishing 80% of the population, although that figure has to include avid movie goers who attended the cinema more than once in a given week. Stories of the panic caused by Columbia Broadcasting System's transmission of the radio adaptation of H. G. Wells' *The War of the Worlds* are now, of course, legendary.

Studies have shown that the viewer's subjectivity comes strongly to the fore when exposed to a film, and there is no real consensus as to what message, if any, can be gleaned from a storyline. For instance, the impact of television has been described as a 'Frankenstein' abroad in society, in that no post-transmission control can be exerted on the audience and the effect of any message the film tries to convey is largely unknown.

Even if a message is clear it often gets lost in the psychological gap between what the film watcher actually thinks and what he says he thinks.

The only certainty seems to be that the visual media definitely have some sort of effect on us. 'Half the money I spend on advertising is wasted ... ' is the observation attributed to the soap magnate Lord Leverhulme, which finishes, '. . . the trouble is, I don't know which half.'

Yet, advertising, political campaigning and movies all cost millions of pounds to create as they all strive to transmit their own individual messages. There is some agreement that the key is the 'association' with an idea that appeals to the majority of viewers.

In advertising history, Pepsi stood for freedom as surely as movie-goers knew the actor Randolph Scott stood for justice, and once a strong connection had been established, the public appreciated reinforcement of their expectations. And although trends come and go, good versus bad remains a constant. Examples are plentiful.

The punk being encouraged to make Dirty Harry's day beguiles the viewer to see the 'morality' of the unorthodox cop's cause and admire his disdain for conventional police methods. Characters like Harry Callahan have a 'higher' moral code than the rest of us, and they stand out because they are not the sort who meekly wait their turn to take the necessary action. 'Bad guy heroes' are admired for their bravery and skill in carrying out daring heists before heading off into the sun – Fontaine's constant destination was a vague notion about somewhere in South America – to live out the remainder of their days in well-earned luxury.

Most films are directly or indirectly instructive, the best examples being the wartime propaganda type which send out all too obvious messages of ultimate victory should audiences behave in a certain way or stick obstinately to their faith in the cause. Some films set out to change things and go on to achieve their goal; it's said the film *Let Him Have It* from 1991 led to the posthumous 1993 pardon of Derek Bentley for the murder of a police officer in 1952 and there seems to be little doubt that *Apocalypse Now* (1979), carried a highly effective anti-war message. *The Cosby Show* successfully challenged racial stereotypes in its portrayal of a black American upper-middle-class family facing everyday challenges.

Even today's comparatively 'media savvy' audiences prefer their moral messages to be unambiguous, with 'right' *usually* triumphing in the end. The success of the television series *The Sopranos* seems to be based on the enduring fascination of seeing those who live entirely on the wrong side of the law, eventually, and with Shakespearean certainty, coming a cropper. Yet, as can happen when juries in criminal trials see the 'bigger picture', a fair degree of anti-social behaviour is tolerated by viewers without condemnation and without losing faith in the 'message'.

Emotional bias develops in the average viewer who then wills a particular outcome to the story line. But for most, the emotions quickly fade after the film ends and normal life resumes. Some, though, have difficulty distinguishing between reality and fiction and for them there's a deeper, though unintended message, which is carried on into daily life in the shape of unfulfilled dreams and undermined morals.

Fontaine appears to have fallen into the latter category. His sister Violet remembered the powerful effect some films had on her brother and the routine they would have to go through at his insistence when they went to the movies. They were avid film-goers and made a weekly booking at a restaurant before taking in one, or sometimes two, films. On those occasions, he always called her 'Anne', she thought as a reference to 'his older lady' and as they dined he gave her ongoing tuition in what he considered to be restaurant etiquette. Fontaine was enthralled by the movies they saw, particularly those with high-flying, wayward but lovable villains. A particular favourite of his was the plotline involving the gentleman-by-day, thief-by-night alter ego called Raffles.

RAFFLES – A LIFE'S AMBITION

Ernest William Hornung is not as well known as his famous brother-in-law Sir Arthur Conan Doyle, the creator of Sherlock Holmes. Whatever family dynamic might have been at work, Hornung preferred penning stories about a 'raffish' gentleman thief who lived a double life. By day, 'Raffles' was an admired and accomplished cricketer – the sporting pursuit of English gentlemen – and at night, a 'cracksman' who broke into jewellers' shops and made off with fabulous gems, leaving an impertinent calling card for the baffled authorities. Raffles' night-time activities were usually restricted to wealthy, well-insured business premises, but should a close friend be in deep financial difficulties, Raffles would resort to stealing a hostess's diamond necklace to help save him from suicide, or worse, social disgrace.

As Holmes used his extraordinary powers of deduction to battle evil, Raffles charmed his way through wealthy Victorian and Edwardian aristocratic circles impressing the lords with his athletic prowess and fluttering the hearts of the ladies with his debonair demeanour. He would have been the last person suspected of being 'the amateur cracksman' – akin today to tennis ace Roger Federer being an international art thief.

There have been several adaptations of the character down the years, but the one that disproportionately affected Fontaine, according to his sister Violet, was the 1939 film starring David Niven and Olivia de Havilland, Joan Fontaine's sister and bitter Hollywood rival. Clipped English accents and blithe aristocratic mannerisms abound.

Although a jewel thief and cad, Raffles is adored by the victim he steals from, admired by the dogged detective who chases him and loved by the leading lady. But then, he had vowed to give up his nocturnal double life until he heard that his 'fag' and best pal Bunny was about to be cashiered from the Guards should he be unable to repay money he had 'borrowed', so there were deeper principles at stake.

Ultimately, of course, the stolen necklace was returned to Lady Melrose, the reward money went to Bunny and his career was saved. Raffles, meantime, left a tearful leading lady as he naturally honoured an agreement to hand himself in to the police.

In the 1930 adaptation of the story, with Ronald Coleman as lead, Raffles and his lady leave to start a new life in Paris, but the later version was obliged by the censor of the time to impose a more moralistic ending, which showed that crime doesn't pay.

To Raffles, the only thing he could envisage as more exciting than theft was dodging the police. At one stage it occurred to the despondent Bunny that, in effect, he'd 'become a thief', but Raffles responded, 'We're all thieves in different ways!' The message is evident for those 'astute' enough to see it; stealing can be principled and keeping one step ahead of an unimaginative constabulary is really just entertainment.

Numerous 'Raffles' pointers appear throughout Fontaine's narrative. His 'Soviet contact's' secret telephone number ends up being hastily written on a book of matches from the Dorchester; Raffles is linked to Lord and Lady Melrose as their new telephone number is written on a cigarette packet.

Lady Melrose's maid doses her nightcap with an extra sleeping powder so her 'genuinely criminal' accomplice can steal her necklace; Fontaine keeps the tragic Walter Scott-Elliot docile in similar fashion, apparently so he can steal his worldly wealth.

One of Raffles' jewel raids takes place when the shop alarm has been switched off, and Fontaine's absurd story about the raid on 'Gerrards' uses the same technique, albeit the system there was meant to have been remotely disabled by a contact.

Just before the police arrive, Raffles persuades another thief to chloroform him to cover the truth of his involvement in the theft, and Fontaine commits the first chloroform murder in British legal history.

Raffles returns a stolen painting and Fontaine returns a studbook stolen from a horse trainer on the basis it was the 'sporting' thing to do.

One needlessly deferential account of Fontaine's last night of freedom after escaping from the North Berwick police has 'the imperturbable gentleman' not forgetting his 'old world charm' by insisting on paying the fare to the taxi driver whose vehicle he was arrested from at a road block; as he was being arrested at the time, it's hardly likely that the police would stand back to allow him to reach into his pocket for money.

Olivia de Havilland breaks down in tears when Raffles tells her he's no good for her, as Phylis and Margaret and Hazel and Ruth all apparently do when Fontaine does the same thing; there's no suggestion of the infatuated partners feeling sorry for, or being relieved at ridding themselves of, an incorrigible criminal.

Were all these similarities a coincidence or was Fontaine's later behaviour influenced by viewing the film? Did he dream he could live as Raffles did as he and Violet left the cinema and made their way home through the blacked-out Clydeside streets of 1940? It is clear that the film's 'message' did have some long-lasting influence on Fontaine's subsequent behaviour, so what other films might have shaped his abnormal outlook on life?

REBECCA

Fontaine claimed that when he used his adopted surname for the first time, it was simply an impulsive reaction to meeting a more refined character, and was in homage to the great ballerina Dame Margot Fonteyn.

Violet said otherwise. She recalled that he seemed to be deeply affected by the character played by Joan Fontaine in Hitchcock's 1940 adaptation of Daphne du Maurier's story *Rebecca*. In it, Joan Fontaine's character met and married the widowed George Fortescue Maximilian de Winter played by Laurence Olivier. She quickly discovered that not only was she socially out of her depth, but she was very much in the shadow of the first Mrs de Winter, Rebecca. It also looked very much as if de Winter had murdered Rebecca in a fit of temper, but as the plot unfolds, Rebecca is seen to have been unfaithful to de Winter and to have apparently invited her own demise after she discovered she was suffering from a terminal illness. Joan Fontaine's character, simply referred to as the second Mrs de Winter, is tricked and bullied throughout by the pro-Rebecca housekeeper, but the marriage survives whilst the family pile, Manderley, does not, being consumed by fire.

The film showed that as an outsider, the second Mrs de Winter could prevail against the stifling snobbery and deceit that the plutocracy and their lackeys employed to keep her in her place. There does appear to be a fairly glaring 'mixed message', however, in that Olivier's character seems to succeed in getting away with an almost 'justified murder', something that might have later echoes in Roy Fontaine's subsequent career. The acceptable ending was a matter of debate at the time, given the terms of the 'Hays Code' of 1930, which set censorship guidelines for the American film industry. The code had three general principles, the first of which was:

> No picture shall be produced that will lower the moral standards of those who see it. Hence the sympathy of the audience should never be thrown to the side of crime, wrongdoing, evil or sin.

Whilst the code could attempt to 'legislate' for audience reaction, it could, of course never take account of the susceptible individual bent on extracting more 'meaning' than was ever intended by the film's producer.

Should any link exist between Joan Fontaine's surname – inherited from her mother Lilian's stage name – and Roy Fontaine's self-created veneer of refinement, it might simply be that she represented poise, beauty and glamour and stood for all the things a sexually confused and impressionable young man from a working class background might aspire to attain. His underlying sexual uncertainty could also account for him choosing 'Fontaine' above 'Niven' or 'Olivier' or 'Bogart' and could also throw light on his teenage habit of swathing Violet in bedspreads and pinning brooches on her in order that she became 'glamorous', or spending hours making clothes for her dolls.

Whatever effect *Rebecca* and other films of the day had on the young Fontaine, there remains the image of the smug teenager in the 1940s psychiatric ward being assessed by the sceptical psychiatrist. The subject is carefully enunciating his words and looks very pleased with himself, fondly imagining the lady interviewing him is being swept away by his film-star charisma. He had evidently already learned the type of person he wished to emulate, and this charming guise would only develop further from that point on, assuming new aspects that would help Fontaine achieve his envisioned celebrity future.

TURNING THE TABLES

When Fontaine was sentenced to ten years' preventive detention in 1964, the presiding judge listened to the nature of his crimes and then mentioned the role of the 'butler-crook' in theatre lore, particularly in the play *The Last of Mrs Cheyney*, which was made into a 1937 film starring Joan Crawford.

Indeed, Mr Edward Clarke QC was spot on with this comparison. The plot involved a team of jewel thieves headed by the American 'Mrs Cheyney', who quickly endeared herself to polite English society. Having succeeded in stealing a duchess's pearl necklace, she ultimately gave up her life of crime to marry one of the lords who had been obstinately pursuing her. The real hero, however, was the butler, Charles, who had made a career of relieving the titled classes of their expensive accoutrements by way of 'charm and manners' rather than violence. In the end, he handed himself in to the police, thus allowing Mrs Cheyney to marry and bring her criminal past to an end, hence the title.

Before that, though, Mrs Cheyney turned the tables on the hypocritical toffs by *insisting* that they call the police after she had been caught in the act. At first the gentry debated, 'What are we going to do with her?' but, realising the hypocrisy of their lifestyle, one of their number eventually asked, 'What is she going to do with us?' This caused Charles the butler to remark that he would never have allowed the future Mrs Cheyney to stay overnight with them if he had known what sort of people *they* were!

Though a professional thief, the butler emerges as the hero. He ultimately holds the moral initiative and has the vision the gentry lack to see beyond the limits of the pettiness and self-ishness their wealth has brought them.

In addition to the justification of stealing from the rich, the sexual appeal of the criminal's lifestyle was also echoed in many of the popular films of Fontaine's day. In Hitchcock's 1955 film *To Catch A Thief*, Cary Grant had to continually fend off spell-bound women who found his former profession of jewel thief hugely alluring. Ultimately, though, the upper-crust Grace Kelly succeeded in catching him, proving perhaps that the best way forward for a future man of the world was a history of theft.

Other probable film references in Fontaine's story appear frequently. For instance, in the Lady Aylwen scene, where the foreplay consisted of her summoning him repeatedly to her bedroom prior to her proprietorial demands for sexual satis-faction, her stated resemblance to Dietrich and the sensuous cigarette smoking was highly reminiscent of the famous actress's stereotypical image.

The 'shooting party' cover story for Wright's murder has all the signs of a film plot not quite matching *The Trouble With Harry* from 1955, in which a rabbit hunter came to believe he might have accidentally shot the deceased; in a later scene, the body is placed in a bath. The scene in *Kind Hearts and Coronets* from 1949 where the immaculate Dennis Price shoots the trapped Alec Guinness also has some similarities. Indeed, there are several instances in Fontaine's memoirs which conjure up Price's image, including apologising to robbery victims who have suddenly realised he was not from the CID, or when he was caught *in flagrante* with the Swedish maid and, having attended to his state of undress, coolly asked for a month's pay as a condition of leaving.

Fontaine's affectionate recollection of 'Captain Jackobosky' appears to be a reference to the 1958 film *Me And The Colonel*, in which the humble but resourceful Jewish refugee Jacobowsky, played by Danny Kaye, teamed up with an arrogant Polish officer, Colonel Prokoszny, and his beautiful French girlfriend in occupied France. They all somehow managed to keep one step ahead of the approaching Nazis, inevitably, in a vintage Rolls-Royce. The meek fugitive's imaginative forethought continually kept the party out of danger, despite the pig-headedness of the strutting, aristocratic Pole played by Curd Jürgens. Fontaine's memory of 'Jackobosky' appears to be a fantasy fusion of the parts Fontaine found attractive from both characters.

The basis for pretending he had successfully played out 'The Sheik' routine might possibly arise from the famous film of that name from 1921, in which a headstrong western woman eventually succumbs to Valentino, as Sheik Ahmed, after he rescues her from the evil Sheik Omair. The film's release led to general female hysteria at cinemas and widespread disdain from possibly jealous males who accused Valentino of looking effeminate and too pretty to be a 'proper' man. It is thus open to conjecture how the film impacted the young Fontaine, with its hero conveying all the traits he so wished to emulate, and led to his later life fantasy.

Of course, the effect a film has on the vast majority of viewers is temporary. The entire audience can live vicarious lives of excitement, love or glamour for the film's duration but very few of them tend to become jewel thieves after watching *Ruffles* or enlist in the Mafia after seeing a few episodes of *The Sopranos*. For some, however, there's a compulsion to take things further than most of us would think reasonable or rational.

Studies show that a link exists between a reliance on film media for information and the propensity for criminal behaviour, the greater the reliance, the greater the possibility. Put another way, the loner who gets most of his 'socialisation' from the movies is going to be out of step with the rest of society to a greater degree, and it goes without saying that the effect is greatly magnified if there is already some mental imbalance.

While that certainly seems to have applied to Fontaine, there are other known examples. John Hinckley was convinced that his attempt to murder President Reagan would impress Jodie Foster and would lead to him having a relationship with the female star of *Taxi Driver*. American serial killer Joel Rifkin, who murdered seventeen women between 1989 and 1993, was said to be infatuated by Hitchcock's 1972 film *Frenzy*, from which he gleaned some practical hints about the mechanics of murder. When eventually arrested, he was found to have Noxzema cream smeared on his moustache to combat the stench of the decaying corpse found in the back of his pick-up truck, an idea imported from the 1991 film *The Silence of the Lambs*. Undoubtedly, then, Fontaine was neither the first nor the last case of such media-inspired delusions. The other examples also demonstrate how easily the already unbalanced mind can be influenced and even informed by what is meant to stay in the world of fiction.

SEEKING AN IDENTITY

Hero worship of film stars, rock bands or top sports personalities is, of course, commonplace. For some people, though, it goes much further than that.

When Mark David Chapman shot John Lennon dead in New York in 1980, he claimed he had heard voices telling him to 'do it, do it, do it' just before he pulled the trigger. Chapman, who failed to gain parole in his sixth hearing in September 2010, also said he had been influenced by religious feelings that encouraged him to get rid of someone who regarded himself as 'bigger than Jesus'. Psychiatrists, however, found Chapman's quest for identity a more compelling explanation, with him usurping his former idol Lennon's identity and becoming 'someone' in his own right in the time it took to fire four shots into the musician's back.

Perhaps the clearest examples of just how far impressionable fans are capable of going come from rock music. Heavy metal band Judas Priest were sued in Reno, Nevada, by the parents of two fans who alleged that their sons had shot themselves as a result of listening to the band's music. Nineteen-year-old Ray Belknap had shot and killed himself, then his friend James Vance used the same shotgun to blow half his face away – he survived for three further years, horribly disfigured – because of a repeated subliminal command 'do it' which appeared in the band's version of 'Better By You, Better Than Me'. Vance explained he had no wish to die but as the music had driven them crazy, they had no control over themselves. In short, the band had murdered his friend Ray.

The attorney for the families argued that Judas Priest were responsible for placing 'that kernel of encouragement' in their recording, whilst the band argued there was no such command and in any event, what were listeners being encouraged to do? Make a cup of tea? Mow the lawn? Given their choice of commands, the band members were said to have favoured, 'Buy more of our recordings.'

In what would appear to have been a compromise ruling, the judge claimed he *could* hear the 'do it' order in the tune when it was played backwards, but held that the juxtaposition of the words 'do' and 'it' was unintentional and dismissed the case, thus leaving unanswered the question as to how far a band can be held responsible for the reaction of their fans to their music. The lead singer, Rob Halford, also pointed out that the tune was actually a cover version of one originally written by a member of the band Spooky Tooth. Halford went on to ask that if the judgement went against them, what would the ramifications have been for the band Suicidal Tendencies? The same could also have been asked for films like *Kill Bill*.

Put another way, in the unlikely event of Vance v Judas Priest becoming a persuasive precedent, would it be possible for the relatives of Roy Fontaine's victims to raise a class action in the United States suing Joan Fontaine, or the estates of Sam Wood, the director of *Raffles*, or Alfred Hitchcock, the director of *Rebecca*?

Probably not, but confusing film plots with reality seems to have been only one strand in Fontaine's psyche, as he also undoubtedly developed other sociopathic traits which are common to his kind.

38

WAS HE THE CLASSIC PSYCHOPATH?

REARING A MONSTER

It is said that some future sociopaths are encouraged to develop their egocentric behaviour by one of their parents over-indulging them to the extent that the child then fails to properly distinguish between right and wrong. Serial killer Andrew Cunanan was said to have an overdeveloped sense of what was due to him as a result of his parents pampering him, but when his father left he felt outraged by the supposed rejection and from then on suffered fits of extreme jealousy.

It is certainly true that the Hall family was not a happy one. Writing during his final spell of incarceration, Fontaine recorded that his mother was 'a beautiful spirited woman' whom he would 'be close to all his life', but his father was something of an unimaginative religious man whose authority he quickly overcame when he was only sixteen. Put another way, Marion had encouraged, assisted in, and benefited from her son's numerous thefts, whilst Archibald had been hopelessly undermined on the few occasions he had attempted to discipline the young Fontaine.

By the time Wootton met the Hall family in 1952, the father, he recalled, was a friendly host but it soon became clear his family had no respect for him. Marion had been affable to the point that she not only became upset when Wootton left, but she also even suggested they run off together, which they did shortly thereafter. When she left Archibald she took Donald with her, and she and Wootton went to a girls' school in Dunblane, Marion as cook and Wootton as gardener.

Whatever problem was at the root of her marriage to Archibald, her decision to run off with Wootton seems to have come as a major surprise to both her husband and her daughter, neither of whom were aware of any genuine difficulties in the marriage. Marion obviously thought otherwise, but had kept it to herself.

There was clearly some dark secret at the heart of the family. Despite Archibald being Violet's adoptive father, and Fontaine later claiming that Archibald wasn't Donald's father either (though that has to be seen in the context of his 'justifying' Donald's murder), subsequent events suggest that Marion was at the root of the problem. Not only did Marion seem to enjoy undermining her first husband Archibald, but her unpredictable disposition seems to have cowed both of her husbands into instant submission, which contrasts sharply with her *laissez faire* approach to her firstborn's early criminality. Did he have some sort of emotional hold over her?

At one stage, long before Fontaine's violent character fully erupted, she confessed she was 'terrified' that her son would physically assault her. By contrast, she was protective of Donald and regularly complained he was being badly treated by other family members, particularly Fontaine. Her attitude towards her adopted daughter Violet seems to have swung between welcoming acceptance and strident rejection. After Marion ran off with Wootton, Violet eventually had to resort to tracing her mother herself, there being no suggestion of contact otherwise.

Perhaps Marion recognised in Fontaine the same personality disorder that had caused her own mother to be admitted to an asylum in 1938 where she remained until her death in 1955; records no longer exist and there is a suggestion that Marion's mother might have been an epilepsy sufferer, but the length of her stay would indicate otherwise. If so, and aware that she was the conduit between the two, Marion might have come to regret her early indulgence of her son as she eventually recognised Fontaine's potential for violence and began to fear him.

Yet Marion was no angel herself. She had been dissatisfied with her husband, yielding to yet frightened of her first son, indifferent towards her adopted daughter and protective towards her second son, and despite having run off with Wootton, she never seems to have found the happiness she imagined was just round the corner. Her proto-hippy attitude had palled in later life and she became troublesome, difficult and prone to terrible mood swings, depression and violent outbursts.

Another illuminating fact is that, while her marriage certificate states that she was twenty-two when she married Archibald in 1924, her death notice records her year of birth as 1912, so she was either seventy-three when she died in 1975 or twelve when she married in 1924.

Perhaps Fontaine gained from his mother a tendency to adorn and exaggerate situations in order to put himself in a better light, which having gone unchecked at home, later developed into serious fantasy and disengagement from realistic understanding. The history of mental illness and Marion's own restless and eventually violent disposition certainly sheds light on the dangerous traits Fontaine apparently inherited.

Archibald senior, on the other hand, emerges as the well-meaning, but ultimately ineffectual character in the Hall family history. By the time of his death in June 1962, Fontaine's father had at least kept his religious faith as his private life crumbled around him. Marion had, of course, run off with Wootton, and he had little or no contact with his family, except for Violet who sometimes made the effort to visit him. Donald had been the focus of police interest from an early age and was often in trouble with the police for various mindless thefts in England.

When Archibald died, he lived alone in Park Road in Glasgow's West End, but the death was registered by an old friend from Haddington in East Lothian. Despite everything, Archibald did not forget his two sons; in his will he left £670 and out of that left £250 to each of them. The local Lansdowne church received £25 but there was nothing, surprisingly, for daughter Violet and nothing, less surprisingly, for his estranged wife Marion.

Violet, however, was understanding of his motives. She knew her father was hoping that the meagre sum he left to his sons might help establish them on a more 'righteous' path. Even the hand-written terms of the will showed a remarkable level of understanding, considering the trying circumstances his family had put him in.

His firstborn son is referred to as 'Roy Fontaine Hall' and his address as care of Violet's home address in Newcastle-under-Lyme, Staffordshire, despite Archibald knowing that Fontaine was in prison again when the will was drafted in 1961. Nevertheless, there is something quite poignant about the father's misguided hope that the small sums he was able to leave to his dangerous firstborn and his feckless second might make them see the error of their ways.

If Archibald had been granted a divine preview of what was to come after his death, though, even he might have relinquished all hope. Fontaine had been allowed to attend the funeral unescorted, and had, amazingly, measured up to the trust placed in him by the prison governor by returning to prison at the agreed time. Fontaine claimed he felt 'shock' when he heard the news of his father's death, but, notwithstanding his distress, he typically conspired with Marion so she could pilfer from Archibald's flat. Whilst the son asked pointless questions of the solicitor handling the estate, the estranged wife wandered round the flat helping herself.

Marion had married Wootton on 23 March 1963, nine months after her first husband died. Archibald had steadfastly refused to contemplate divorce, probably just for appearances' sake, although a sad and totally unrealistic dream of salvation and family togetherness on his part cannot be completely discounted.

The terms of Archibald's will reflect the hopes of a forlorn but distant father hoping to save his sons from the uncertain futures to which their chosen paths were leading them, but

Marion's own demise released an intriguing piece of information from Fontaine that may shed further light on their warped family dynamic. Wootton recalled Fontaine's first visit to his mother's grave after she succumbed to cancer in 1975 when he told Wootton he was sorry for all the trouble he had caused her. At a subsequent visit in January 1978 – by which time he had killed four people and was only days away from murdering the brother Marion so carefully shielded – he said something strange. Placing an expensive bouquet on the grave, he spoke to his deceased mother, saying that *she* knew what he had done and he was sorry for it. Wootton asked what he meant but he said he couldn't tell him, but, *'She knew.'*

Had some dreadful taboo been breached or was he simply trying to be his usual mysterious self? Maybe Marion's tactic of encouraging her son to undermine her first husband developed far more than she could have ever wanted it to. Whatever happened, Marion took the secret to her grave.

Fontaine's adopted sister Violet also appears to have been a close confidante. The two were close during childhood – going to the cinema and to restaurants together – but Violet also remained in touch with Fontaine throughout his criminal career. In a *Raffles*-type scene, she recalled seeing the jewels from the Mowbray House job in a basket in their London flat, just as the police came to the door. She supposedly then covered it with a towel, took it from the house and hailed a taxi to the nearest tube station where, by chance, she saw Fontaine in the street. She then threw the basket to him and returned to the flat. A rather far-fetched story, suggesting perhaps that Violet was prone to spells of exaggeration similar to those of her brother.

Also, Violet seems to have had some involvement in Fontaine's attempt to dredge up publicity after his imprisonment in 1978 with his story about there being 'other bodies'. She claimed to have 'found' the letter Fontaine had 'left' at her house around Christmas Day 1977, weeks before he was arrested and before the money-making plan had been hatched. It would almost seem that Violet was used to this behaviour and she was only doing what she always did – playing her role in another of her brother's enigmatic schemes. Fontaine was certainly skilled in employing anyone who could be of use to him.

Whatever the truth behind these complex family relationships, it appears that Fontaine and Marion had a secret that was sinister enough even for him to keep quiet about. Perhaps they were trying to mask a different family revelation altogether. The unspoken 'secret' between Marion and Fontaine supposedly related to something *he* had done which only she knew about; further speculation could easily revolve around a possible secret *she* had which only he knew about – or Archibald senior chose never to mention – namely the question of paternity. Not, as Fontaine loudly proclaimed, the paternity of brother Donald – 'the skinny child of a minuscule Army major' – but the question of the identity of his own father. Of possible but admittedly limited significance is the fact that Donald was given Marion's maiden name 'McMillan' *and* his father's middle name 'Thomson' as his middle names, something that might not have been accorded to a child from 'the wrong side of the blanket' in 1941.

Moreover, when Archibald senior made his will in 1961, he deliberately mentioned Donald – who by that stage had also gone off the rails, so it probably was not done to register disapproval – *before* his putative firstborn son. Whilst acknowledging that neither of these hypotheses are particularly persuasive, the reaction serial killer Ted Bundy had to discovering that his grandparents were not his parents and his 'sister' was in fact his mother is often cited as at least one of the root causes of his subsequent murderous rampage. Fontaine's fulminations about not having the same father as Donald may simply be a reaction, then smokescreen, to the truth.

And if that was the case, it may reveal the rationale behind his rejection of his given name and use of various aliases throughout his life. In truth, it would make sense that Fontaine used such multiple personae to mask a deeper identity crisis – both paternally and sexually. It does seem that when the homosexual side of his character was in the ascendancy – as it usually was – he was 'Roy Fontaine' and when he was in the process of courting a woman or recalling earlier heterosexual pleasures he was 'Roy Philips'.

Beyond the direct influences of his family members, there are other factors that point to possible trauma in Fontaine's childhood. For example, Archibald senior's tactic of moving house whenever his son showed signs of wrongdoing could have actually been based on sound reasoning, the boy's effeminate tendencies most likely finding little sympathy in playgrounds populated by boys raised in the bloody lore of the Great War. It would be a major surprise if the child who became Roy Fontaine was *not* bullied at some stage – as many up-and-coming psychopaths are – requiring his parents to seek out continual 'fresh starts' in different areas of the city. It would be even harder to believe that such harassment would not have had a profound effect on him, leading him to be an ostensibly non-violent fantasist whose later revenge was to be cold-hearted and pitiless towards those who either upset him or were simply in a weaker position than he was.

Although much speculation can arise from an investigation into Fontaine's upbringing, any theories are necessarily only based on what can be gleaned from contemporary sources and other commentators' opinions. Whilst it may be tempting to try to understand Fontaine's psychopathic tendencies using one possible explanation or another, it would be unwise to read too much into any of his versions of events. Even Fontaine's unquestioning and reliable factotum, John Wootton, admitted: 'If he told me he was going south, I would naturally assume he was heading in the opposite direction. He is that kind of man. Everything has to be devious and everything he said was full of innuendo.'

Whether the trauma was committed within the family or without, there is no doubt that Fontaine was hiding something deep within his psyche. Clues might even be found in his eccentric spelling and grammar. *A Perfect Gentleman* abounds with misspellings of names: 'Wright' when he means 'Wight', 'Esther' when he means 'Esta', 'Kirkleton' when he means 'Kirtleton' and so on. He could not possibly have written his own references and these may have been done by Wootton, who surprisingly appears to have been both legible and careful in his script – if a letter he wrote to Lord Grant asking him to reconsider the sentence he passed on 'his son' in 1966 is anything to go by. Nevertheless, it's been said that an analysis of Fontaine's handwriting discloses a confused, self-centred and arrogant personality that masks a deep-seated sense of inferiority.

IT'S NEVER THE PSYCHOPATH'S FAULT

As a child, Fontaine said, he was bright and good at school and could have chosen any career. Instead, he chose not to live an ordinary humdrum existence as he was 'born with' an appreciation of jewels and thus preferred to become a thief.

No suggestion, then, that he was simply a sneak thief who stole anything he could, no matter the value.

Why go to the bother of pretending that what he did was anything other than lowlife crime? For him, the suggestion that the route his life took was somehow a choice he made due to inborn talent is a blatant attempt to 'legitimise' his crimes. Having typical psychopathic disdain for others' intelligence, there was no consideration of legitimately earned possessions; all of his victims were privileged and thus deserved to be robbed. He later maintained, when working for the Law family, that had he been born to their wealth, *he would not have become a thief*. In that case, had he been born to wealth and able to legally obtain the jewels that so enticed him, can it be assumed he would have understood those who stole from *him*?

Reinforcement of Fontaine's 'legitimacy' for his life of crime comes from his attempts to persuade the reader that he was in fact a man of culture and principle. He acts fairly if treated fairly, so returns to prison after his father's funeral having given his word to the governor that he would. He hates sadists and rapists, looks after friends and pregnant women, finds it impossible to steal from certain people, reluctantly takes a deal offered by the prosecution which goes easy on friends and relatives but makes it harder on him, and pays a fair price to fellow thieves for their unwanted stolen goods. Whilst criminal colleagues indulge in vulgar, working-class pastimes, he goes off to galleries and Turkish baths, and police chiefs recognise his refined philosophy when they confide their pleasure that it was he who committed the crime and not 'some foreigner'.

Further justification for theft comes from statements like 'people wanted to associate with you', 'women like men who are not pulled by society's strings' and 'some scams were based on the victim's greed' – all observations designed to minimise the perpetrator's guilt.

It's highly unlikely that Fontaine even thought about joining the Merchant Navy – he would have been in custody of one form or another during the latter part of the Second World War – but, according to Fontaine, they too have to accept that their rejection of him after a week's training led to him having no option but to continue breaking into houses.

And how badly did British justice treat him? Whilst he got what amounted to a life sentence for understandable, insurance-covered, violence-free thefts from wealthy people, a paedophile that same day got a mere six years!

He and others risked life and limb bravely speaking up against a corrupt warder in Parkhurst but the authorities wangled an acquittal; throughout the tale he makes no mention of having the second key to the records office, or of his attempts to sell another inmate's records.

Prison brutality hardens a man and shapes him for what he does in the future; the warders at Parkhurst in the 1960s have to bear a large responsibility for the murders he committed in 1977 and 1978.

Yet, no murders would have happened if fate hadn't made him 'find true love' in Barnard only to have him killed in a car crash, causing Fontaine's disregard for life. Had Barnard lived, there was talk of going into business together and living a crime-free life – no mention of Barnard choosing to ignore him on his release. Indeed, in the earlier publications there was no suggestion that Barnard was either the 'love of his life' or even that he had tragically died driving the very vehicle his devoted amour had so generously gifted to him.

As for David Wright, he gave Fontaine no alternative but to kill him, stupidly attempting blackmail then threatening to murder him, forcing Fontaine to defend himself by shooting Wright first.

And had Wright not been killed, no one else would have been, so in effect Wright's greed was to blame for three of the other four deaths, Kitto alone being responsible for the murder of Mrs Scott-Elliot. Being from a lower criminal league, Kitto had tried to impress Fontaine by attacking Mrs Scott-Elliot, which ran contrary to Fontaine's plan to leave the Scott-Elliots 'skint but alive'.

After she had been killed, Walter Scott-Elliot also had to go, as his appearance without his wife would alert the authorities.

Mary? Greed was her downfall and her boasting was dangerous for Fontaine's continued freedom.

Donald deserved to die; he was only a half-brother but was a despicable, weak, slovenly character who would have had designs on Fontaine's daughter if he could have gained access to her in Fontaine's enforced absence. Even he, though, contributed to his own downfall by trying to assure Fontaine of his own criminal prowess with his demonstration of how to tie victims up using the minimum amount of string.

Ultimately, though, Fontaine's own downfall was due mainly to Kitto's incompetence in not changing the car number plates properly, although it has to be said there was also an element of Basil Fawlty-style suspicion on Mr Wight's part which inspired him to call the police.

In short, Fontaine chose an almost legitimate, glamorous path but the actions of others left him with no option but to get deeper and deeper into crime. As for the murders, he really had little or no responsibility for any of them, the victims dying through a combination of fateful but lethal circumstances that were out of his control.

THE ALL-IMPORTANT FANTASY

Rather than 'Fonteyn' – after Dame Margot – he really became 'Fontaine' – after Joan – so why pretend otherwise? Sometimes, and for no obvious advantage or material gain, the psychopath does irrational and contradictory things, either to ensure he's noticed or to make it seem he's cleverer than he really is. He's even capable of doing things that are clearly against his interests as long as he gains attention, and all of his actions are subject to instant whimsical change, as if he's guided only by what makes him feel good at any given moment. The whole elaborate charade is designed to forbid the outsider from ever really knowing what is truly going on inside, and to mask deep-rooted feelings of worthlessness.

Fontaine once gave his coat to a tramp in the presence of a lady friend, always gave generous tips to staff in bars and restaurants, and was in the habit of buying raffle tickets for good causes; none of these acts were down to his generosity but were in the nature of payments in exchange for attention. In fact, he could 'write off' such losses by mean, clandestine behaviour even against his own family.

Around Christmas 1977, he fooled his great friend Wootton into selling Mrs Scott-Elliot's mink. The coat Mary had become so dangerously attached to was passed off as one of Ruth's possessions, which, inexplicably, had been given to him as part of their 'separation' agreement. Wootton advertised it in a local paper and subsequently sold it for £200.

The impertinence of such behaviour should come as no surprise.

Taking a stolen artefact to Esta Henry's son seems absurd, incomprehensible and bound to lead to police interest, but was possibly calculated to confuse the ordinary mortal and simultaneously add mystique to his reputation. *Perhaps he's been misjudged and is an antiques expert after all?*

Supposed cries of, 'Good luck, lads!' from fishermen on the banks of the river to Fontaine and the two others, whom they recognised as escapees from Blundeston Prison, further illustrates the fantasy being played out. Given the danger they would have posed to their community, would three local men seriously wish desperate convicts well?

And returning the genie to the bottle is impossible; once the charade is launched on the public, there's no way back. When an unsuspecting victim apparently goes along with the early stages of the pretence, the fantasist regards it as 'confirmation' of his delusional belief.

Michael Newitt appeared at Leicester Crown court in 2008 and was sentenced to two years for fraud after he tried to convince creditors they should quietly write off his debts, on the basis that he was an undercover security operative. Good work if you can get away with it, but the trouble was that Newitt actually believed he was a commander with MI5 and had a fake ID card made up, awarding himself the equally fake honour 'CMG', which had been awarded to James Bond in the film *From Russia With Love*. He had blue lights and a siren fitted to his car and stopped suspected drink-drivers before calling for police back-up and handing them over. Even his ex-wife thought he had a top security post at one stage, but in court he was described as a man of low self-esteem whose principal aim was *not* to commit crime but to 'generate respect'.

Samuel Blair Cowden was a fantasist who travelled all over Britain in the 1970s and 1980s craving respect. His *modus operandi* was so unique that he was instantly identifiable by the nature of the crimes. His cover was to arrive at the victim's door and somehow be able to talk knowledgably about the family's relatives in Australia, whom he claimed were friends or neighbours of his 'Down Under'. He explained he had emigrated some years before, had become a successful accountant and was on a short holiday back in the United Kingdom. Anxious to befriend him, the householders often made him a meal and he would stay for as long as six hours chatting about their relations in Perth or Adelaide or Melbourne.

The sting came when he was leaving and he 'discovered' that his secretary in Australia had forgotten to give him a new cheque-book; usually he would be given small amounts to tide him over until the next day, when he said he would repay the house-holder's kindness by buying them lunch in the five-star hotel he was staying in. When the family contacted the hotel the following day, of course, they were told no one by the name they had been given was staying there. Some victims suspected he was bogus after a while but when his financial requests were so low, they gave him the benefit of the doubt and decided he might be genuine.

Given the amount of money spent on the expensive suit, coat and briefcase, as well as the effort of both researching the victim's family tree and applying the false tan he wore, the whole exercise could hardly have been cost-effective, on top of which he was of course the subject of an arrest warrant as soon as the matter was reported. He craved acceptance more than money. The strength of the fantasy sometimes overcomes all other considerations, even to the exclusion of fleecing the victim for as much as possible.

Fontaine's proven activities are redolent with puzzling behavioural quirks; why should he stop for lunch with Mrs Scott-Elliot's body in the boot of the car, or book into a hotel and enjoy food and drink whilst his brother's corpse was outside in the hired car with the false registration plates?

Esta Henry confirmed before her death in a Brazilian air crash in 1961 that Fontaine *did* visit her shop with a bunch of roses after the 1953 theft, and Lady Hudson was startled to find a Christmas card and a present for her dog arriving in time for Christmas 1977; she might have been even more unsettled to find out Fontaine was proposing that his ashes eventually be scattered on her Kirtleton Estate. His other request at that time was that when *The Daily Telegraph* published his obituary, they should note that his name was 'Roy Fontaine'. He couldn't care – or simply hadn't realised – that both of these latter proposals might cause offence.

Prior to the shock of the 'natural life' term imposed at the Old Bailey in 1978 – most others would have expected it – he proposed holding a 'celebration dinner' at the Savoy to commemorate his release earlier that year from the fifteen years imposed at Edinburgh. Whilst that may have been a rare moment of levity on his part, who can be certain?

Copeland, the author of *The Prison Cell Confessions of Archibald Thompson Hall*, recorded an interesting insight when Fontaine told him they would have got on well had they met 'outside'. The sentiment was quickly qualified when Fontaine added, 'but I don't suppose we would have been mixing in the same circles,' and it's to be assumed that Fontaine meant the author rather than the killer would have been in the lower echelon.

All of these bizarre actions give further confirmation to his perception that mere mortals are amenable to the notion that he had not *actually* done very much wrong. It never occurred to him that the associated glamour from jewel theft exists only in fiction and that any public 'admiration' for well-executed gem heists or bank raids is necessarily limited.

And anyway, for the psychopath, there is only one person who matters – himself. Because of that, he seeks the limelight and enjoys attention, but should others go along with his self-perception, it only adds confirmation to his belief. Of course the Chief Constable of Edinburgh should meet his train after he was arrested for the Mowbray House raid, and naturally the Commander of Special Branch should want to personally interview someone as significant as him after he was charged with the theft of government papers. Both of them wanted to shake his hand as well, probably in recognition of the fact that, after all, it's just a game of cat and mouse between him and the authorities, who tacitly concede he really *is* the important human being he so desperately wants to be.

39

OR WAS HE MAD?

Fontaine's wife Ruth said her husband claimed he had been influenced by 'The Beast' Aleister Crowley, who died in 1947 aged seventy-two. Attempting to define what Crowley stood for is not easy, but in the course of his life he was a writer, a poet, an occultist, a British spy, a mountaineer and, strangest of all, a Jacobite, and was known as 'The Wickedest Man in the World', an epithet earned *without* apparently committing any murders.

Crowley proposed his cosmic philosophy 'Thelema' as the 'religion of the new epoch' with the central tenet being 'Do As Thou Wilt'. As a British spy conspiring to bring America into the Great War on the Allied side, he had no difficulty exercising the necessary 'flexible morality' required for the task, something he had honed throughout his life pursuing his constant desire to shock the conventional middle classes. Apart from a disdain for traditional religion, the abuse of drugs and an unconventional sex life, the two had little in common and the notion that Fontaine had the desire or intellectual ability to espouse – or understand – Thelema seems hugely unlikely. It would seem that his shallow espousal of some of Crowley's beliefs acted as a convenient mantle, which he sought to use to wrap up the glaring oddities of his own troubled psyche. Of the two of them, very few would be able to allege that Crowley was in greater need of psychiatric care than Fontaine ever was.

As a matter of routine, a murder accused is examined to find out if he is sane and fit to plead, to find out if he understands the charge he faces and if he can give proper instructions to his legal representatives. Fontaine's previous psychiatric history was carefully assessed in 1978 when he was indicted for murder in both Edinburgh and London and he was found to have a 'grossly psychopathic personality with marked criminal tendencies'. Following his arrest in January of that year, his psychiatric interview took place shortly after he had emerged from a coma, brought on by his suicide bid from barbiturate overdose. In such circumstances, it might be anticipated that the subject would be listless and depressed, particularly if the will to live had all but disappeared.

Not so with Fontaine.

He was energetic and lively and spent almost all of the first two hours of the interview on his favourite topic – himself. The interviewer, like his professional colleague nearly thirty years before, found Fontaine 'superficially pleasant' to the point of ingratiating and once he started talking, he required virtually no further prompting. Even with the passing of all those intervening years, Fontaine still believed he could charm the hardheaded professionals whose purpose was to assess him, rather than be impressed by him.

His 1981 biographer, Copeland, also recorded that when he first met Fontaine in prison, he greeted him like a friend from long ago, asking after his family and complaining that it had been such a long time since they had seen each other. Copeland was initially puzzled, as none of his family had had the dubious privilege before, but it quickly became evident that Fontaine employed the same false routine with everyone he met.

In 1978, Fontaine told a psychiatrist that he had attempted suicide as he had been responsible for *six* murders and felt ending his life was the only way out. Despite having only just emerged from a coma, he appears to have been in a resurgent frame of mind and anxious to maximise his mystique as well as his bank balance. He had been directly involved in five murders but had taken judicial blame for four, although his later invention of two more killings seems to have been designed for the dual purpose of obliging the authorities to check his claims, and exploiting the culture of chequebook journalism which existed at the time.

Sometimes what might be seen as his true feelings emerged in the course of the web of lies he spun at the interview. He narrated yet another version of the murder of David Wright in the course of which he let slip he had 'strong feelings' for him, and the mention yet again of Wright's gold Dunhill lighter and cigarettes suggests some hidden significance, possibly other than the 'trophy' theory.

He described his brother as a 'pervert' and rationalised his murder as necessary after an incident one weekend, when his 'half-brother Reginald' stayed with him and his daughter, and was heard to make suggestive comments about her; Fontaine realised that 'if he was ever in prison again', 'Reginald' would be her next of kin, so he was forced to act promptly. Why Donald became 'Reginald' is puzzling – perhaps Fontaine thought he was maintaining his self-imposed standard of not appearing to 'grass' on others. It is true that, having murdered four people by the time he was confronted with the decision to kill Donald, there was a cast-iron likelihood that he would be in prison for the rest of his life, but why 'Reginald' would become Caroline's guardian above Wootton or Violet is not explained.

He accounted for his early psychiatric assessments from the 1940s as being false and due to advice given by an 'astute lawyer' as he went through court – the legal representative had apparently managed to persuade a psychiatrist that the young Fontaine had a mental illness. As a result, he said, he spent six weeks wandering about the hospital before escaping, and claimed he had never been in any mental home before or since. Indeed, he explained, he had been in Perth Prison instead of Perth Asylum.

His solicitor 'persuading' a psychiatrist that his client's mental state required institutional treatment is a novel situation, and possibly the first and only occasion that a psychiatrist has based an opinion of an inmate on something he was told by a third party rather than his own observations of the subject.

Fontaine went on to allege that amphetamines had been

199

introduced into his food by the prison authorities, causing him to suffer a delirious episode and, as there had been a suggestion of a similar episode in Woodilee Hospital in the 1940s, it was thought that at least some of his behaviour could have been drug-induced. Accordingly, it was decided that a urine sample be taken to check for any evidence of amphetamine. However, no further mention was made of it, and it seems likely that Fontaine's consumption of drugs was recreational and its effects were compounded by, rather than the cause of, his psychiatric problems.

It would seem that even as a teenager he was already using his 'banking' technique, evading detection of drugs by hiding them intimately. Then, foreshadowing the Parkhurst warder case, he quickly alleged that the authorities had been responsible for something he alone had done, namely the consumption of the proscribed drugs he had managed to smuggle into prison.

His first admission to a mental hospital in August 1941 was occasioned by bizarre behaviour in prison, but this seems to have rapidly improved in the hospital ward from which he escaped a few weeks later. A later admission to Hawkhead Hospital noted he was suffering from an attack of 'moral imbecility', a phrase presumably covering a multitude of situations, which lasted for an entire week. Whatever an attack of 'moral imbecility lasting an entire week' entails, he was sufficiently compos mentis to escape on 13 March 1943 due to his 'eluding the vigilance of the attendant'.

One of the physicians in the 1940s thought Fontaine was possibly suffering from *dementia praecox*, a term which applied to a condition often affecting young men and which later described schizophrenia. The 1978 psychiatric interviews, however, found no signs of psychotic illness, and, as the symptoms of schizophrenia are self-reported, there seems to be every reason to trust the conclusions of the later reports.

40

THE JUDGEMENT TO COME

Serial killers, it is said, are generally younger than thirty-five. At fifty-three at the time of his first killing, Fontaine was obviously older than the average but it's unlikely he committed any killings before that of David Wright in 1977 for the simple reason that he would inevitably have boasted about it when he was eventually arrested.

Prior to the abolition of capital punishment in 1960s Britain, Scottish criminal courts had developed certain inbuilt safeguards to try to ensure that no mentally ill prisoner was executed, and care was taken to try to categorise any mental disorders diagnosed. Psychotic behaviour – where the prisoner appears to be genuinely out of touch with the realities of everyday life, either at the time of the offence or at the trial – could lead to acquittal on grounds of insanity, but at no stage did the law regard a psychopathic personality disorder as insanity *per se*. At its highest, psychopathy might be seen as mitigatory and lay the foundation for avoiding execution, for instance, on grounds of diminished responsibility. In Fontaine's case, his ability not just to function in the course of everyday matters, but to go on to charm and inveigle his way into butlers' posts and the affections of seemingly sensible women, clearly points more to cunning than to social and emotional dysfunction. Even so, he was undoubtedly delusional to greater or lesser degrees during certain periods of his life, and it has to be wondered how a court that had the power of life or death over him would have resolved the matter had his crimes occurred twenty years earlier.

Whatever influenced him to a lifetime of crime – insanity or psychopathy – it does seem that an escalating pattern can be detected where he progressed from petty theft to break-ins to the fraud of acting as a butler and so on to murder. He makes no attempt to explain his convictions for the possession of firearms in 1956 and 1973, probably because his faith in becoming the celebrated jewel thief of his childhood dreams still existed even then, the guns being part of the default plan he was later forced to resort to when it was becoming clear that a smattering of etiquette was only bringing in petty rewards and colossal custodial sentences. His propensity for murder to further his plans had probably existed from the start, so it was ironic that the killing of Wright probably had more to do with jealousy than with any dark hints of exposure to his titled employer. He had simply become frustrated and time was passing rapidly.

In the end, Fontaine's crimes partially secured him something of the reputation he so eagerly desired, thanks to both his own efforts and the willfully blind sensationalism of some sections of the press. As surely as mud sticks, repeated reference to a self-created status develops in the conversation and minds of others; after a while it can be 'confirmed' by many and by the time the press take up the story, it's fact. Fontaine's acting even fooled otherwise level-headed people, at least to begin with. His wife Ruth does seem to have been temporarily duped and Hazel Patterson was hoodwinked for even longer. And, despite the fact that his domestic posts, as with his romances, usually lasted only briefly, that was not the point – that he got them in the first place at least shows an ability to play a role in the short term.

To his sister Violet he remained a beloved brother and she always forgave him, even after his callous killings came to light. In fact, he appears to have made a particular effort to put on a show in order to try to convince her, himself or both of them that he had somehow made good. This was perhaps best seen around Christmas 1977, when he phoned Violet to explain that the Scott-Elliots were 'spending Christmas in Italy' and although he had been asked to accompany them, he preferred to spend time with his family. The last time that had happened had been Christmas 1952, so Violet – ever the willing foil – was honoured by his apparent consideration.

He also explained that he was bringing 'Robin', his partner in their antiques business, and Violet was delighted. Before they arrived, though, Violet's husband John Harvey phoned Fontaine to tell him that his sister, Margaret, was dying of terminal cancer. Instead of changing the plans to visit, Fontaine immediately left London so as to be near to the family in their time of need; when she died a few days later he seemed genuinely upset at the passing of a mother of two at the age of only forty-nine. At the funeral, Fontaine was tact itself and Kitto served food and drink to the mourners, causing some of them to think that the stranger amongst them was an employee of the funeral directors.

To boost her spirits, Fontaine and Kitto took Violet on a shopping spree where they bought her perfume and earrings and all the food for the Christmas dinner. On Christmas Day, as Fontaine put the finishing touches to the festive table, Kitto again busied himself serving drinks to the various guests. They appeared extremely thoughtful, buying expensive gifts for the Harveys and their daughter Melanie, and John and Caroline Wootton. The afternoon was a major success.

The day ended with the party moving on to the hotel the two men were staying at and images of Fontaine's charm and generosity, as he stood at the bar lighting his cigars with his trademark gold Dunhill lighter, were to remain with those present. No one would have guessed they were responsible for the murder of the woman whose body was discovered that Christmas Day, just as no one would have any idea they had also mercilessly murdered and disposed of an elderly couple and were on the verge of killing Violet's other brother Donald.

But then Violet obviously saw what she wanted to. She had wondered about the Christmas card 'Robin' Kitto had sent her; that it was signed 'Robin Bastard' caused her only momentary perplexity. When Fontaine phoned Violet from the Mount Royal Hotel in London's Marble Arch to discover that Margaret had died, would it have mattered that she knew Fontaine had signed in to the hotel as her husband John Harvey, as he so often did? And of course, at that stage, Wootton was unaware that Fontaine had stolen his credit card and duped him into selling the dangerous mink coat.

Fontaine's 'affection' for his family was clearly as shallow as a puddle. The psychopath only has loyalty to himself and his wants.

Yet, with the benefit of hindsight, John Harvey later expressed outrage at the sheer nerve of Fontaine and Kitto even visiting his house at Christmas time that year. He did think it curious, though, that when Fontaine visited his dying sister in hospital, she regained consciousness for the first time in hours and then, being unable to speak, fixed Fontaine with an unwavering stare. It was as if Margaret had some deathbed insight into his earthly crimes, or had been given the power to detect evil. Whatever it was, Fontaine's carefully maintained veneer of charm had been punctured, he had been seen for what he was and he was temporarily rattled.

For, even if Leopold and Loeb's defence attorney Clarence Darrow had it right when he declared that, 'the prolonged suffering of years of confinement may well be the severest form of retribution and expiation,' one can't help but ponder whether the best way out for someone like Fontaine *would* have been taking 'a pill and a glass of wine'. Perhaps Fontaine's reflections when he explained why he had come off his hunger strike in 1979 held a significant truth: 'Maybe it was the haunting hallucinatory faces of my victims. Who knows what judgement I will receive, when I finally depart this world. I dread to think my torment will continue.'

BIBLIOGRAPHY

Baatz, S. *For the Thrill of It*. Harper Perennial, 2009.

Beltrami, J. *A Deadly Innocence*. Mainstream Publishing (Edinburgh), 1989.

Bone, J. and R. Johnson. *Understanding the Film*. National Textbook Company, 1993.

Copeland, J. *The Butler: The Prison Cell Confessions of Archibald Thompson Hall*. Granada Publishing Limited, 1981.

Dickens, H. *The Films of Marlene Dietrich*. Citadel Press, 1974.

Hagan, F. E. *Introduction to Criminology*. Wadsworth Group, 2002.

Hall, R. A. *A Perfect Gentleman*. Blake Publishing Ltd, 1999.

— *To Kill and Kill Again*. Blake Publishing Ltd, 2002.

Jenkins, R. *Churchill*. Pan Books, 2002.

Kennedy, L. *A Presumption of Innocence*. Victor Gollancz Ltd, 1976.

Lucas, N. and P. Davies. *Monster Butler*. George Weidenfield & Nicolson Limited, 1990.

Lewis, J. *The Ideological Octopus*. Routledge, 1991.

Meehan, P. *Framed by M.I.5*. Badger Moon Publishers, 1989.

Pearson, J. *The Cult of Violence*. Orion, 2001.

Rafter, N. *Shots in the Mirror*. Oxford University Press, 2006.

Spence, R. B. *Secret Agent 666*. Feral House, 2008.

Wansell, G. *Terence Rattigan*. Fourth Estate, 1995.

Wheen, F. *The Soul of Indiscretion*. Fourth Estate, 2001.

Whigham, C. *Olivia and Joan*. New English Library, 1984.

Wood, T. and D. Johnston. *The World's End*. Birlinn Limited, 2008.